The things I did.

At the time it never seemed so bad. In fact it was good. Brilliant. Every day with the lads. Drinking and drinking and drinking and having a laugh. I was what we did. We were a bunch of lads and we were a part of a team. And there is no team to compare. Lads in football teams and rugby teams muck about and have a laugh. They get hammered after the game and take the piss out of each other. Why not? It's what lads do. They pay their subs and in return they get to play a game and have a laugh and get plastered together at the end of it. But footballers and rugby players only get to meet up a couple of times a week. Training on a Tuesday night and a match on the weekend. My team was a 24/7 team. And we played the ultimate extreme sport where mistakes meant a whole lot more than two points dropped. Mistakes meant a pal got dropped.

Dropped like a sack of spuds onto a cracked Belfast pavement whilst all the women would come out to their front gates and bang their dustbin lids in celebration. Up on Turf Lodge I once saw two women up gobbing away whilst their two three year old daughters banged a dustbin lid on the concrete. They should have been playing with Barbie dolls. Instead they banged the dustbin lid. Two of them. Neither was strong enough to lift the thing on their own.

Crash, bang.

The Argyles are here. On the pavement. By the wall. Maybe one of them will get nutted and get their face painted up on the side of a house. Another dead squaddie to add to the mural of Private Builey.

So this is where I go every night. Back there. Back then. Days of rain and the crash of dustbin lids. You know that feeling when you on a big dipper at a fairground? You go up and up really, really slowly. Higher and higher and you know exactly what's coming because you've watched it from the queue for tickets. Up and up and the top is getting closer and closer. And you can't help but get to wondering why the hell you have shelled out on a ticket to ride? But what can you do? There's no getting off. There's nowhere to get off. You look down from the side of the car and it's one hell of a drop. So you take deep breaths and make damn sure that nobody can see that you're whacking it.

Up and up. And the wheels go clack, clack;

Clack, clack.

And the top is really, really close. And you know exactly what is coming next. Sure as night follows day. And you grip the rail in front of you as tight as you can and get braced for it.

You know that feeling don't you? Locked in and helpless. No going back. No getting off. No choice in the matter.

Well that's my life. It's been my life for the last twenty six years. My days are like being in that rollercoaster car. Up and up and up. Clack, clack. Higher and higher. Grip the rail. Grit the teeth. Because the night always comes. You can't stop it coming. And no matter how hard you try and stop yourself from falling to sleep, in the end your eyes will close. Once upon a time I would hoover up lines of speed and coke to stay awake. I wanted to stay awake forever. I still want to stay awake forever. I want to stop the rollercoaster in its tracks and slowly reverse it back to the start of the ride.

So that I can get off.

So that I can have that normal life that everyone talks about.

So that I can stop being an Argyll.

But you can't stop the night. Like they say. As sure as night follows day. Night follows day. And eyes get heavy. Clack, clack. Up and up. Heavier and heavier. Clack, clack.

And all of a sudden sleep has ambushed me like a team of Provos in a disused factory.

And all of a sudden I'm back in uniform again. Back on the Shankill Rd. Back on Turf Lodge. Things we saw. Things we did. The crash of dustbin lids and body parts on the floor.

All those things we saw. All those things we did. Things I saw. Things I did. Endlessly repeated episodes on some obscure satellite channel. What's on tonight guys? Taggart. For the nine hundred and fourteenth time. Maybe there might just be someone out there who hasn't seen that episode already. Maybe there is somebody out there who has been collecting butterflies in the jungles of Borneo for the last twenty years. So what's on tonight? It's Willie on the Shankill Rd. It's Willie on Turf Lodge. Always the same old episodes. Like Fawlty Towers I suppose. They stopped making any new episodes way back in the 1980's and now they just show the old stuff over and over again. Willie on the Shankill. Willie on Turf Lodge.

The worst of it is that the video player in my brain never shows any of the good stuff. When we all laughed so hard that it seemed like someone would be sick. When we pissed about and played cards and hit the town. Those tapes have all been shredded. Whoever is in charge of the video player in my head never bothers with any of that stuff. They only ever play the bad stuff. Over and over and over again.

It's been playing for twenty six years now. As sure as night follows day. Willie on the Shankill. Willie on Turf Lodge. Things we saw. Things we did. Over and over.

So what do I do?

Well what would you do?

I try to make it go away. I try to find a blank screen instead of a screen that shows videos of crashing dustbin lids and body parts on the floor. I try to yank the plug out of the wall. I try to switch off the power at the mains. I try to make everything into a pit of complete and utter darkness and quiet.

It's a place called oblivion and the way to find it is alcohol. It's what I do. Every day. For hour after hour I work my way down to the bottom of the bottle. And then the next bottle. Steady and patient. And sometimes it works and I fade out into a quiet black place where the dustbin lids are far, far away. And sometimes it doesn't work and I still wind up back on the Shankill and Turf Lodge. But even then it is easier. Better to deal with. Less sharp. More blurred. And when I wake up I am bathed in sweat and jumpy as a cat.

Ready for a drink. The first drink. And I get up to start the process all over again. Bottle after bottle. Hour after hour. Getting ready for the night. Clack,clack. Another night. Dulling my senses. Seeking oblivion.

When was the last time I dared to go to sleep sober? Can't remember.

How was it? Don't ask. Don't go there. I'm not going there. Not any more. No way. And maybe that means that you are looking down at me right now. Judging. Maybe sneering. Maybe you might consider me to be pathetic. Just look at him. Hiding away at the bottom of a bottle. Needs to find a bit of backbone. Needs to get a grip. Needs to shape up. Needs to snap out of it. Well, judge me if you like. Makes no difference to me. You see, you don't understand. Not many do. I have given up trying to explain it. What's the point? Instead I seek out others who once wore uniform. Others who saw things and did things. Others who can't lock it all away in a box in the attic and throw a way the key and get on with so called normal life.

And yeah, I don't go out much.

I stay in and I drink. Carefully. Steadily, And if I get lucky, I get to find oblivion for a few hours. And if I'm not so lucky, I get to watch those same old videos. At least I know what is going on now. Thanks to Hollybush House. Will it stop? Probably not. Will it get any better? Probably not.

When I became a soldier I was eighteen and I had no idea how long I would stay a soldier. Nobody told me it would be forever. Nine years in uniform. And then the rest of my life. Night after night after night. Clack, clack. Willie on the Shankill. Willie on Turf Lodge.

And every night the dark hours echo to the sound of crashing dustbin lids.

What are you Willie?

I'm a soldier. An Argyll. For now and for ever and ever.

Amen

Like I said before, I was 18 when I joined up. Have you been watching 'Life on Mars'? If you have, then you will be able to picture the times well enough. Flared trousers and kipper ties. The Bay City Rollers and lots of strikes. And umpteen thousand Jocks on the pitch at Wembley, most with sideburns. I wasn't your stereotype squaddie. I wasn't a schemie with a long rap sheet. Anything but. I was the youngest of four and the older three were all sisters who spoiled me rotten. I was a quiet sort of lad to be honest. I never went out much and never got in bother. I jacked school when I was fifteen and drifted from job to job without ever really settling on any kind of career. Shops and factories. Nothing to write home about. Then when I was eighteen everything changed. My mum was taken into hospital with kidney problems and stayed there for many months. I just assumed that all was well and that she would be fixed. It certainly seemed that way when I went to visit. Nobody chose to tell me that the kidney problems were terminal and so when she died it hit me like a roadside bomb. More than anything else, I was angry to have been kept in the dark like some kid in short pants. Things between me and my dad had never been great. I resented always being told what to do and he was the kind of guy who always told me what to do. All of a sudden I was angry with everyone and everything. Angry with my mum for leaving. Angry with the family for not letting me on the secret. Angry with my dad because I was always angry with my dad. I wanted out. Out of the family home, out of Falkirk, out of my nothing much jobs.

So I joined up.

Like you do.

Join the army and see the world. I'm sure that was the TV jingle in those distant days of Donny Osmond and Hillman Avengers.

Oh yeah. I nearly forgot. You're not going to believe this. I never drank. Seriously. Not a drop. In fact it was no big deal. My mum and dad never drank. Nobody in my family drank. So neither did I.

I actually went all the way through basic without having a drink. After the runs and drills, the lads would pile into the Naafi to get tanked up whilst I would just sit there and drink juice. Unbelievable really. I soon found that being a soldier was something I could be pretty good at. I'm a big guy, six three in my socks, and I have always been pretty fit. I tended to be one of the guys out at the front when we did the big runs.

So I passed Basic and then it was off to join the Battalion in Osnabruck. Like they said, join the army and see the world. Start with the Federal Republic of West Germany. Of course those were the lost days of the Cold War. Somewhere out to the east of the fence, the ranks of the Red Army were waiting patiently to swarm into the West to welcome us all into their socialist paradise. Every May Day they would parade their weaponry in front of a bunch of grey faced guys in fur hats on the Kremlin balcony. On and on they came. Tanks and rocket launchers and thousands upon thousands of hard faced infantrymen. If they had ever come, it would have been like World War Three. Sorry about that.

But of course they never came. More to the point it never really looked like they were going to come. So we didn't have a great deal to do. Our job was to sit about in camp and take part in a couple of exercises a year. Long, slow days.

And I soon learned that life with the Battalion was very different to basic training. Not drinking wasn't an option any more. Drinking was part of the furniture. Drinking was what we did. It was expected. It was normal. If you didn't drink, you were tagged as a 'sweetie boy'. Well I hadn't signed up to be a 'sweetie boy'. So I joined the club and then some. Looking back, it was hardly surprising that we hit the bottle as hard as we did. Every day was filled with empty hours and spirits were stacked high in the Naafi and easily affordable at £1 a litre. Soon I was pissed up every day. Four of us would club together and pick up two litre bottles of vodka, a litre of Bacardi and a bottle of Cola and sling the whole lot into a fire bucket and the drain it.

That was to get us in the mood for going out. Not just weekends and bank holidays. Every day. When we went out on exercises we would fill up our canteens with whisky and vodka. Who needed water? There was always plenty of water on the APC's. And we would all be pissed up as we practiced what we would do to stop the Red Army dead in its tracks. Hell, maybe we might have even managed it. One thing is for certain. That lot would have been every bit as pissed as we were. The only difference would have been that their tipple of choice would have been anti freeze drained out of their T62 battle tanks. Was anyone bothered by the fact that we were all pissed all of the time? Not really. Not at all in fact. There was the odd rumour about a place near Dortmund known as 'The church'. Sometimes guys who had been hitting the bottle harder than most disappeared to 'The Church' for a month or so. We never thought much of it. Many years later I learned that 'The Church' was some kind of in house army detox.

Germany was great. Day after day of getting plastered and mucking about. I started to learn all about pranks. Soldier's pranks. The sort of stuff that can make civvies shake their heads and look troubled. Like the time when a new green behind ears lad from England somewhere joined us. We took the mattress off his bed and tied him down tight to the wire. Then we put and iron on his chest, switched it on, plugged it, in and left him. He screamed like a stuck pig and we laughed our socks off. We had removed the fuses you see, and the searing pain that made him scream was all in his imagination. The next day he thought it was funny too. It was just the way it was. Was anyone bothered? Of course they weren't. Because the British Army has always thrived on humour in the face of disaster. There is an old tale from the trenches that has wandered down the years. Is it true? Maybe. Probably. A Jock regiment is ordered over the top. Out they jump, kilts on and the piper giving it his every breath. The Germans machine gunners open up and scythe down half the company in a matter of seconds. Retreat! Get back! Bloody hell. Then word comes forward from the country house ten miles back. Awfully sorry chaps, but your country needs you to give it another bash. Another charge with the piper making the mud of Flanders sound like a small piece of Scotland. And the Germans open up again and another half of the company is shredded. Retreat! Get back! Bloody hell. And yet again the word comes forward that they need to go again. At which point one of the squaddies turns to the piper and says 'For Christ's sake man, can you no' play something the bastards like!"

Army humour.

Gallows humour.

If you don't laugh you cry. Don't I ever know that. As soon as I stopped laughing I started crying and I have been crying ever since.

After five months it was time to up sticks and head across the water to Ireland for some real soldiering. Join the Army and see world. Osnabruck to the Shankill Rd. For a while, me and a few of the younger lads laid off the booze and went into full on serious mode. This was showtime. The real deal. We would head out patrol crouching and moving and doing everything by the book. And the older lads would get pissed up and laugh at our earnest enthusiasm.

Then it all changed at the end of a night patrol. The wee small hours of the morning when the whole wide world is fast asleep. Orange street lamps. Gurgling gutters. A radio crackling. The sound of boots on concrete. Another alleyway. Bins. Litter. And something on the floor.

The something was a someone.

A very dead someone with his throat cut through to the spine. And it wasn't like the movies. A body in an alley on a dark Belfast night.

Ever heard of the Shankill Butchers? Lenny Murphy and his band of psychos? Maybe not. It's kind of typical of how things were in those crazy times. Lenny and his boys butchered over thirty people in the 1970's. The Shankill Butchers were technically part of the UVF, but in reality they were little more than complete and utter lunatics who plumbed the depths of evil. Murphy would take a ride into Catholic areas in his mate's taxi and they would grab anyone they could lay their hands on. The postcode was all he needed to make up his mind that a pedestrian was a Catholic. They would take their victim back to a basement in a drinking den and butcher them. At the time, the press at home was filled with stories of the Yorkshire Ripper. So Murphy went about his killing spree and nobody seemed to notice much. The RUC never managed to arrest him. He met his maker care of an IRA nutting squad in 1982.

I was nothing more than a bit part player in all this. The 19 year old Jock on a long night patrol through the empty echoing streets. The 19 year old Jock who found the slashed up body in the alley. And what did the army have to say to me about it all? Nothing of course. Just go and have a drink lad. Forget it. Wipe it. And I was quiet happy to take their advice.

And so it was back to the tried and trusted Osnabruck routine. Muck about and get hammered. All day. Every day. In the base we would sit around and play cards and drink. Then it would be time get kitted up and go out on patrol. Night patrol meant calling into the pubs and clubs to see if we could spot 'faces'. Well that was how it must have looked on paper. In reality we would all pitch up at the UDA club on the Shankill and leave our guns and flak jackets and caps behind the bar. Then it would be free drinks and plenty of them. I remember half crawling out of that bar one night so drunk I was literally dragging my weapon on the ground behind me. Back to base. So drunk we could barely walk at times. Then we would be debriefed and it was plainly obvious that we were smashed. Was anyone bothered? Of course they weren't. It was how the army got by on the streets and fields of Ulster. We got drunk and we stayed drunk and when we saw some bad stuff we got even drunker. And made a joke of it all.

Another night patrol.

Some lads going down the Shankill.

Other lads going down the alley that ran parallel. The back of a bar. Bins. No windows. No lights. All quiet. My brain mushy and fuzzy from all the booze. My pal spots a pair of boots sticking out from under a pile of boxes. He goes over to give the boots a kick. But the boots don't move like he thought they would move because there are still feet in the boots. And to go with the feet there is a whole body except there isn't much of a head there at all. It's all smashed to bits. Almost obliterated. Later it turned out that they had been doing some kind of weapons inspection and one of the players had managed to shoot himself in the head by accident. Yeah, well, that was what they said. They had a board meeting about it and decided that before they dumped the body they best get the bullet out. No doubt the bullet would have told a forensic story they didn't want to be told. So they decided to get it out. Like you do. But these lads were not working in a lab off 'Silent Witness'. No scrubbed floors and fancy equipment. They were in a Shankill basement and they had to use their initiative. So they used it. In fact they used a beer keg to smash open the skull so that they could dig out the bullet. Then they smashed it up some more so that nobody would be able to tell what had gone down. Then they must have dumped the body outside in the back yard ready for someone to collect it and take it away to be buried somewhere.

And then we came along and buggered the whole thing up. Someone tried to cover the corpse with a pile of empty cardboard boxes but he never used enough to cover up the boots.

Not that I knew any of this. Why should I? I was just the nineteen year old Jock who found the corpse with the head that was barely a head any more. You all right Willie? Course you are. Not to worry. Get yourself back to base. Have a drink. Have ten drinks. Twenty. Whatever you need. Things will look different in the morning. They always do. On you go.

Click.

Main menu.

Click

Scene selection.

Click.

The city centre now. Night dark. Air cold. Situation normal. All the pubs are long closed and we are the last men on earth. Just the sound of heavy boots on the pavement and the distant sound of thin traffic.

Until there is another sound. Close by somewhere. Down an alley. Always down an alley. A barely human shape down on the floor. Moaning. A horrible moaning that gets stronger as we draw nearer with our guns up. Guns ready. Heads swimming. Torchlight. And the figure of a man jumps into focus amidst all the litter in the alley. He's a man in a pool of blood with four holes in him. One through his left elbow. One through his right elbow. One through his left knee. One through his right knee. Pale face stretched tight.

And moaning in pain. Not howling. Not screaming. Just a horrible, desperate moaning. And the moaning had got stronger with every step we took down the alley. Want to know why that was? It was the sound of the boots. The footsteps. You see, he didn't think it was us. He must have had his eyes screwed shut against the pain and terror. He thought we were them you see. Them. Bakers and wagon drivers and brickies. Back to put a hot one through the back of his head. Back to put his lights out. For what? Well what would I know? I was just the nineteen year old who staggered through those dark Belfast streets with a live weapon and a spinning head. They didn't bother to give us the big picture. What was the point? We were all so pissed that Page 3 of the Sun was hard enough to focus on.

We walked from A to B.

We followed our orders.

We got by.

Click.

Main Menu…..

Are you with me so far? Is any of this making any sense? Are you about to say that you understand? Maybe you are. Because in a way, all of this is logical enough. You take an 18 year old from Falkirk and put him in a dark alley with a dead guy with a big gap where his throat is supposed to be and it is going to leave some poison to fester away in the brain. Does your brain compute that? Does that explain why the big guy you saw sitting on his own in the pub the other day suddenly burst into tears for no apparent reason and legged it out of the back door looking embarrassed and ashamed?

Is it enough for you to nod and say I understand, Willie. Christ that must have been rough, Willie.

The problem is that it is not always that easy. I don't much want to tell you the next thing. And you probably don't much want to read it. Because here is where the black and white ends and the grey starts. Will you still say that you understand? Maybe you will. If you do then, I fear that you have been to the same dark places that I have been. The bad places where we do bad things.

Things that all these years later we can't believe we did. Things we don't know how we did. Things that seemed to make sense at the time and make no sense at all anymore. Things that we want to lock down forever and forever. Out of sight is out of mind. Lift the carpet and sweep and sweep and sweep….

Before I go there I want to remind you of how it was. How utterly crazy the world had become. Lunatic. Senseless.

I was just a lad. Not an excuse, just a statement of fact. I had become a part of the ultimate team where we dealt with danger and boredom by getting drunk all day every day. A team that moved like ghosts through the dark streets of a strange, dark city where sometimes we tripped over guys with no throats and no heads. And if we hadn't laughed we would have cried. So we got drunk all the time and we laughed at stupid stuff. And maybe you can imagine the kind of hate that was in the damp Belfast air back then. It was a hate that had been hundreds of years in the making. Hate that lay behind three year old girls crashing dustbin lids. Hate that lay behind a guy having his throat slashed to the spine. And in the middle of all this festering hate was a bunch of pissed up young Jocks with live weapons and orders to move from A to B. And then from B to A. There and back and then back to the camp for a laugh. For a session.

Can you begin to get your head around what happened to our heads?

So remember the thing with the iron on the lad's chest with the fuses taken out? Where did that stand with you? Close to the line? Over the line? Acceptable? Unacceptable? Blurred?

And where is the line? And how do you see the line when you are young and confused and drunk all the time? How do you remember what is OK and what is not OK? And who is there to tell you? And when is it really not OK to make a joke of it? And why?

Confused?

I was confused.

I'm still confused. I'm always confused.

Clack, clack.

So anyway, one day we had to take some completed paperwork back to base. A few hours earlier a car full of Provos had been clocked. They had been about to get out. They had weapons. Outside a school. The lads who had spotted them turned whole thing into a rerun of that last scene in 'Bonnie and Clyde'. Christ knows how many rounds they put into that car. Plenty. More than plenty.

And now the car had been brought back to base for forensic examination. Not the bodies. They had been taken somewhere else. But there were still plenty of body parts plastered about what was left of that riddled car. Bits of skull bone. Bits of brain. And we were drawn to it. Like kids. Like stupid, stupid kids.

One of the lads reached in and picked up a bit of skull bone and pocketed it. Why? Christ knows why. Later he drilled a hole in it and threaded it with string and wore it round his neck. Why? I don't know. He didn't know. Nobody ever does.

So what did I do? I had a packet of fags in my pocket. There were two left. I took them out and put them in another pocket. And then I reached inside that car and picked up a lump of brain.

And I put it in the fag packet.

And I put the fag packet back in my pocket.

A bit of brain.

Are you still going to nod at me with sympathy in your eyes and say that you understand?

So the next day we're on road block duty. Can you open the boot please sir? Can you get out of the car please sir? Can we see some identification please sir? We are going to search you now madam.

But of course it wasn't for us to search a female suspect. That was against regulations. Only female soldiers searched female suspects. Fair enough. So when we did roadblock duty, there was always a female soldier along with us. And what do young lads to when they are around young lasses, especially when they are drunk? They piss around. They show off. They act stupid.

But where is the line? And who is there to explain where the line is?

We got into our car and started back to the base. I was sitting next to the female soldier. And I offered her a fag. And she reached in without looking first. And you know exactly what her fingers touched.

And I cracked up.

And the lads in the front of the vehicle cracked up.

And she cracked up.

Except that she cracked up in a different way. She screamed like the demons of hell were all over her and she started to open the back door to get out even though we were going fast.

Drag her back. Drag her back. Close the door. Not so funny anymore. Nobody's laughing anymore.

Shit.

Christ.

But where was the line?

Did I do that?

Was it really me?

Clack,clack.

Over and over and over and over….

Why?

Don't ask me why. I don't understand why. Or how. And is it any wonder that I burst into tears for no reason whatsoever? Is it any surprise that sleep equals horror. Every time. Do you still understand? Of course you don't. I don't. Nobody does.

Oh we see it on the news of course. In Bosnia and Rwanda and the market places in Baghdad. How? Why? What makes men like that? Where was the line?

All I know is that I went there. Over the line. Young and drunk and confused and scared and stupid. And nobody told me it was bad. They just said have another Willie. Forget about it Willie. Get on with it. Get by. Go from A to B.

People talk about the thousand yard stare. They wonder where it comes from. Well this is where it comes from.

Did I do that?

Why did I do that?

How could I have done that?

Been there.

Seen it.

Been a part of it.

And why did it seem to be OK at the time? And why is it not OK any more?

And all I want to do is to forget and forget and forget.

Bury it deep. Wipe it clean.

Make it go away.

But it never, ever goes away.

Clack, clack.

Every night every night every night every night every night.....

And so I drink.

The event that changed everything came from nowhere. We were far away from the dark back alleys of Belfast. Instead it was the rolling hills of the New Territories in Hong Kong. They call the Argyles 'The Thin Red line'. Well it didn't get much thinner when you think about it. The battalion on one side of the wire, and a billion Chinese on the other. So no problem there then.

One morning we were off out on a run. This was 1979. I was always one of the fit lads which meant I would be one of two places on a run. Sometimes I would be out front setting the pace. Other times they would put me at the back to kick the slow lads up the arse. On this day I was at the back.

Runs were for everyone including cooks. One of the cooks was finding it hard. At first he stayed up near with the front, but not for long. Soon the rest of the column moved past him and he found himself right at the back.

With me.

And I did my job. I screamed at him. I pushed him. I dragged him. I abused him.

Eventually he went down. Red faced and overheated and gasping and broken.

Then the sergeant came along and screamed at him and kicked him but none of it did any good. The lad was knackered. So we rolled him to the side of the track and left him to sort himself out. We'd get him on the way back.

But when we reached the spot on the way back he wasn't there any more. Gone. Fair enough. He must have got himself back together and headed back to the camp.

We got back and cracked a few cans to kill the hours until the evening patrol. Early in the evening some officers appeared and asked me questions about the run. Nothing complicated. I gave them the answers they needed and they said cheers mate and that was that. Hang on a sec. What's this all about? Why all the questions? What's happened?

Oh. You didn't know then? It was that cook. He died you see. Heat exhaustion.

If I hadn't asked they wouldn't have told me. Why would they? Who was I?

I kind of sleepwalked to the Naafi and bought a whole crate of beer and sat down on a balcony to work my way through it. Later, all the lads got geared up and headed out on the patrol. Nobody asked me if I was going. It was just assumed that I wouldn't be going. It was just assumed that I would sit on the balcony and drink myself senseless. Which I did. The next day was just like any other day and nobody ever said a word about the dead cook.

The dead cook who I killed.

Years passed and in 1982 I hung up my uniform after nine years. It was time to join the rest of mankind in the pursuit of a normal life. Leaving was odd. It was a case of out of the gates and onto the bus. Nothing was said. Just like the day I killed the cook.

But things were OK and for a while my life was very much normal. A job, a family, a house. Sure, work seemed boring. And at times life seemed boring. But that was OK. In the evenings I would have a couple of cans in front of the TV. These days it is all about units. Keep a drink diary and count the units. Then you compare the number of units you have put down your neck with the maximum number you should have put down your neck and then you think bloody hell fire.

But for two years after I left the army, my drinks diary would have been right in the zone. Sensible. Normal. And there seemed no reason why the remainder of my life shouldn't have been the same.

Sensible.

Normal.

Until everything changed.

I supposed it was a bit like getting run over. One moment it is just another moment in a completely ordinary day. The next minute the car you have failed to spot has knocked you up in the air and ruptured all your internal organs and broken your bones.

And after that nanosecond, you will never be the same again.

In the blink of an eye you have become a different person. A damaged person.

Permanently.

I was channel hopping. Barely watching any of it. Winding down to bed. The remote took me to the end of a Granada programme. And all of a sudden what was on the screen jumped across the living room and slammed into me like a rubber bullet.

The story of a dead cook.

An army cook. Heat exhaustion. Hong Kong. 1979. Left alone to die. Bullied and abused to his grave. I worked out that the programme was all about peacetime deaths in the Army. Were they avoidable? Was casual brutality endemic? Was the Army at fault?

I grabbed the phone and got through to Granada. I told them it was me. I was the one who killed the cook. The one in the programme. Was there anything I could do? Did the family want me to be a witness? Could I have a telephone number for the family?

No I couldn't.

But they promised to pass along my details and in the end the cook's brother called me up and we talked. Then nothing.

Except it wasn't.

The shock of seeing the story of the cook on the TV had opened up a locked cupboard somewhere in one of the back rooms of my brain.

And it started.

Nightmares. Outbursts. Uncontrollable tears.

Clack, clack.

Willie on the Shankill.

Willie on Turf Lodge.

A pulped head under a pile of boxes. A throat cut to the bone. A fag packet. A dead cook.

Over and over and over and over….

Night after night after night after night…..

For twenty six years.

My family knew when I was about to blow before I knew it myself. It must have been something in my face. In my eyes. I would ask them what it was, but they couldn't really say. I would be just sitting there watching the tele and they would all quietly get up and leave the room. Just like that. Nothing would be said. They would just get up and leave. And then it would hit me. Be all over me. And I would be raging and shouting and totally out of control. Thank Christ my violence was only ever verbal. I never attacked anyone. Why? I don't know why.

Every night brought only nightmares. Every night. Tearing at my soul. Eating away at my resolve. Relentless. Remorseless.

And how did I handle it? You know exactly how I handled it. When in doubt have a drink. Have a bucketful. Write it off. Tomorrow is another day. Screw it. Just get hammered. But by now drinking was different. Gone was the camaraderie of the camps in Osnabruck and Ulster and Hong Kong. Then we would drink together. Drown our sorrows together. Have a laugh together. Fix our wounds together. Wipe the slate clean together.

Drinking alone was darker. More mechanical. Soon oblivion was my only goal. Blackness. Nothingness. Sanctuary from the nightmares. There were no laughs any more. At first I would go to the pub in the hope of finding light and comradeship. But who was there who would understand? Nobody. For them life was all football and what was on the TV and what a bitch that Thatcher was. I felt like the freak in the room. The odd one out. The only one who had been across the line and entered the dark places. Worse still was when I would suddenly burst into tears for no reason. One minute I would be OK. Minding my own business and working my way through a few drinks. The next minute I would be crying like some school girl with a dead puppy. And of course everyone would be looking. Staring. What's with the big man and the tears? And I would get to my feet and get out of there. Totally ashamed.

Over the years everything fell apart. Home. Family. Jobs. Health. The slippery slope. The nightmares were my only constant. And the drink. The rest just collapsed around me. And for twenty endless years I tried to drown it all with can after can. Bottle after bottle. Because I had been told that to show weakness is never an acceptable option. I had had it drummed into me. Again and again and again. Normal people could show weakness. They could find a shoulder to cry on. Not an Argyll. No way. We were the

Thin Red Line. We would take anything the bastards had to throw at us and we would laugh in their faces. Always. Every time. And when it was all done and the ground was strewn with bodies, we would drown it all out in the bar.

Twenty years.

Sliding and sliding and sliding.

Hiding away. Locked into my own vicious circle.

Clack, clack.

Until at last I started to reach out for help. Nervous. So bloody nervous. And there were doctors who would stifle yawns and write scripts for endless bottles of pills. A female head doctor who was young enough to be my daughter who yanked away at the inside of my head. And all of a sudden I knew I was going cry. And how can a lad like me burst into tears in front of a young lass like that? It was against everything I had been taught. It was unacceptable.

So I ran.

Back to the bottle.

Back to my locked down world.

In the end I found salvation of a sort. It is a place called Hollybush House run by Combat Stress. A big house in the Ayrshire countryside where broken soldiers can find some peace for a while. And at last there were people who were able to explain what was wrong with me. Why I would burst into huge rages for no reason. Why I would start crying for no reason. Why every night would take me back into the dark places. PTSD. Post Traumatic Stress Syndrome. They cleared the fog that had choked me for all those years. At last I could understand. And they understood. Because everyone at Hollybush House has been to the same dark places. It is a place where I can be back among my own kind. It is place where I never burst into tears. It is a place that has helped me to learn to live with myself a little better.

So am I fixed?

No. Maybe I'll never be fixed. I still drink all day every day as that car on the big dipper works its way up to the top.

Clack, clack.

Some nights I find oblivion, but only some. Most nights sleep takes me back to the Shankill and Turf Lodge. My kids are back in my life again but my doctor shakes his head when he sees the result of my liver tests.

Maybe my life might continue to get a bit better. Maybe not. Maybe there is a wonder drug around the corner that will draw all the poison from my brain. Maybe the public will learn to understand all the broken soldiers like me a little better. I have made new decisions and I am trying my best to stick with them. It is time to stop hiding and lying. What is the point? What is there to lose?

Mark asked me if I wanted to be anonymous. If I wanted the names and the places changing. But I am done hiding. My name is Willie and I was an Argyll.

I'm still and Argyll.

Always will be. These were some of things I saw and did and every night I pay the price. Judge me if you like. I promise it will be nothing compared to the way I judge myself.

You should know that I am not looking for your sympathy. I am still a part of that Thin Red Line. A broken part. Patched up and barely able to stand. But I am still in the line with all the rest of guys. Eyes forward. Weapons ready. Many of the men might be little more than shells but the line still holds. So sympathy? You must be joking.

I just want somebody out there to listen.

Think about this. After every patrol we would be debriefed. It didn't matter if it was late or raining. It didn't matter if we were all as pissed as rats. There was always a debriefing. And yet when I left the army there was no debriefing.

And I wandered around in the darkness for twenty endless, dismal years until someone explained what the hell was wrong with me.

It doesn't have to be this way. Surely the Army could free up half a day to explain the things might go wrong in a soldier's head in the years to come. They could explain it the army way. Just like stripping down and reassembling a weapon. OK. Listen up. Here are the symptoms… number one……

If you start exhibiting any of these symptoms, then there might be something inside your head that needs attention. If it happens, don't panic. Here's a phone number for Hollybush House. Don't lose it. And then they could show a DVD from Hollybush House. A film including some interviews with guys from all the wars of the last fifty years. Brave men. Great soldiers. Men who have found a way to reach out for a helping hand.

Would my life have been different if I had been shown that DVD back in 1982? Maybe. I like to think that it would have been. Would I have staggered around in the dark for two decades whilst my life collapsed around me? If I had known there was a number to call would I have picked up the telephone?

I think I would have done.

I should have been given a better chance. Being a soldier is all about being told exactly what to do in any given situation. We are shown what to do over and over and over again. So that when something happens in the mayhem of combat, we do the right thing without thinking. Instinctively. For most normal human beings the response to being ambushed is both simple and logical. You work out where the shots are coming from and run like hell in the other direction. Not so us. We are trained to work out where the fire is coming from and charge it. Screaming and showing total aggression. It is completely against every normal human instinct, but we do it because that is the way we have been trained to respond.

Over and over and over again.

Here is the situation and here is how you react. You don't think. You just do.

And it works. Of course it does. The Thin Red Line is still unbroken and it has had plenty thrown at it over the years.

So is it really too much to ask for a few paragraphs to be added to the training manual. If you start to feel like this, then pick up the phone. Your instincts tell you to cover it up and hide it away and put on a brave face. Ignore them. Don't worry about showing weakness. Don't think. Just do. Pick up the phone. Here's the number. Use it.

Well.

I guess that's about it.

A message from Willie?

Sure. Why not?

If you're mind is like my mind, all scrambled up and broken, then pick up the bloody phone and take the help on offer. For Christ's sake don't leave it for twenty years.

If you are a politician or a big wheel at the MOD, then free up some time and cash to give the guys a bit of training before they leave. Tell them the symptoms to look out for. Give them the numbers they need to call. Maybe even give them the chance to talk to some lads like me who waited far too long.

That's it.

I'm done.

I'll pour a drink and light a fag. Check out these words. They are from Black Sabbath's 'Paranoid'.

This is my world.

This is my life.

'Finished with my woman cause she couldn't help me with my mind
People think I'm insane because I am browning all the time

All day long I think of things but nothing seems to satisfy
Think I'll lose my mind if I don't find something to pacify

Can you help me
Thought you were my friend

I need someone to show me the things in life that I can't find
I can't see the things that make true happiness, I must be blind

Make a joke and I will sigh and you will laugh and I will cry
Happiness I cannot feel and love to me is so unreal

And so as you hear these words telling you now of my state
I tell you to enjoy life

I wish I could
But it's too late'

## CHAPTER TWO

## DON

Those of us of a certain age will remember being shown old maps in school history lessons where more than half of the world was coloured in red. It was a while ago, way back in the days when a teacher would belt you around the ear holes if you kicked off and when you got home your dad would tell you that it served you right. And so the author shows his age! I don't suppose they dwell on these maps any more and it is probably for the best.

It was once called the 'Empire on which the sun never set'. The Union Jack fluttered from Aden to Adelaide and from Calcutta to Cape Town. Some of the methods we employed to achieve such extraordinary control over vast areas of the planet are probably best left well alone in dusty old cupboards buried deep in the bowels of Her Majesty's Foreign Office.

Nevertheless, how we managed to achieve such global power still remains a fascinating question. Britain is after all a small and rather wet little island off the coast of Europe. Geography offers no obvious clues as to how such a few people managed to rule the roost over so many. If such a question had been put to an expert in 1850 he would maybe have come up with two simple statements of fact.

Statement one : The Royal Navy rules the waves. All the waves: bar none.

And this of course was true enough. There had been a few close shaves. Trafalgar had been a mighty close run thing and it could have very easily have gone the other way. But of course it didn't go the other way and Nelson got his spot up on the column. Those were the days when our Navy was wrapped in a cloak of invincibility and my how we played on it. Those were the days of gunboat diplomacy when if anyone kicked off anywhere where the map was coloured red, a gunboat would be dispatched to teach the pesky blighters a lesson. The Germans were so in awe of the reputation of the Royal Navy in the First World War that they bottled it completely and preferred to sink their ships rather that risk the abject humiliation of having them sunk by us.

Statement two: A British square never breaks.

This was also pretty well true. So what was the much vaunted British Square? It was four lines of soldiers, usually standing two deep and formed up to make the shape a square. The commander and the medics and the quartermasters and all the ammunition would be in the middle of the square. The men who made up the walls of the square would stand tight together.

Shoulder to shoulder. No gaps. They would stare out at the enemy with a calm ferocity and they were trained to be able to stand through absolutely anything. They didn't dive for cover. They didn't duck and weave and give each other supporting fire. They didn't take advantage of any cover that the terrain offered.

They just stood.

Calm and immovable and implacable. And no doubt the Union Jack fluttered alongside the colours of the battalion in the heart of the square. And if any soldier was shot or blown apart by a canon or pole-axed with a lance or half disembowelled by an assegai, then a soldier from the second rank would calmly step forward and fill the gap. The men in the line would wait until the order was given for them to raise their rifles and obliterate the advancing enemy with a murderous fusillade.

These legendary squares worked on several different levels. Of course when they raised their weapons and let loose, the withering fire they released was truly murderous. But more important was the legend we created around the British square. It didn't matter who it was that approached one of our squares, they tended to have lost the battle before a shot was fired. In their heart of hearts, the men who tried to break these squares knew that it was a hopeless task. They all knew the legend. They had heard of the day when the might of Napoleon's elite cavalry divisions had been broken beyond repair on the fields of Waterloo as they were bled white by attacking the British squares over and over again. Likewise the men of the square had been taught that they were part of an unbreakable whole. They were part of a long and proud history. All they had to do was to stand firm. To keep their shape. To follow orders. To keep the upper lip as stiff as a starched collar. To keep face. To be a part of the legend.

Only the new technology of the twentieth century rendered the square obsolete. First there was huge and accurate artillery fire. Then it was Gattling gun. Then tanks, dive bombers, napalm, Hellfire missiles from Predator drones. What chance a square? None.

When was the last stand of an unbroken British Square? I guess it was probably 1895 when the massed cavalry of the Mahdi were cut to pieces in the heat and dust of Sudan. A few years later the hit and run units of the Boers never allowed the British to form their squares in open battle. Then in 1914, the fight against the Kaiser was all about trenches not squares, and human conflict moved to a new industrial era.

And so we come to Don.

For although the squares of the British army disappeared with all those millions upon millions of square miles of red on the map, the mentality behind the squares has lived on down the ages. Because of course when all is said and done, squares are made up of men. Not supermen, but ordinary men. Usually young men from small villages and towns. How was it that such men were able to stand shoulder to shoulder and take whatever was thrown at them? To be so unbreakable? To still stand when their best mate was blown to pieces just inches to their side?

Training and history. Training and training and training. Over and over and over again. Hour upon hour of screaming drill. It is a system that has worked for hundreds of years. Take an ordinary young man and mould him into a cog in the machine. Make him a part of the square. Mould him into a section of a thing that is impossible to break. Is it blind courage or is complete numbness?

Who knows? It is certainly not for me to say.

It is however very much the story of Don. Don has paid the price for what we might call the 'square mentality'. He's still paying the price. When I asked him if he would prefer to remain anonymous he was adamant that it should be so. He explained that talking about the problems that so many try to deal with once they hang up their uniforms is not looked on kindly. Even after twenty seven years, many his old comrades would have no truck whatsoever with anyone making a public show of weakness.

And there of course is the key word.

Weakness.

British squares never break for the simple reason than not one of the men who make up the square ever shows weakness. Not a trace. Should one soldier show any sign of weakness, then it could soon become infectious. One could become two and two could become three. And all of a sudden, the enemies facing the men of the square would sense this weakness like a pack of ferocious wild dogs. And all of a sudden the Union Jack and the colours of the regiment fluttering in the middle of the square would no longer seem like the very symbol of invincibility. And all of a sudden the square of men in red coats would no longer be a thing that was unbreakable. Instead it would become a small group of young men, frightened and hopelessly outnumbered and far, far from home. Vulnerable. Beatable. Ripe to be wiped out.

All of which of course means that it is in the interests of every single man in the square to bury any hint of weakness a mile deep. Their lives depend on holding that calm collective gaze. Calm and unbreakable and bolstered by hundreds of years of history. Not that this is anything new of course. The very same dance was played out at Thermopylae when three hundred Spartans held off the hordes of Xerxes for three blood soaked days. It had been hammered home into the psyche of those Spartans from their boyhood that they were unbreakable so long as they stood shoulder to shoulder and showed no weakness. This belief was so overwhelmingly strong that those three hundred men were able to face down a force of umpteen thousand and still maintain a faith in ultimate victory. On the flip side, the men in the front ranks of the Persian forces must have felt completely doomed as they advanced onto that thin line of blood soaked spears. They would all have heard the legends of the Spartans. At the moment of truth, the fact that they were part of a force of thousands must have meant nothing. And the fact that there were a mere three hundred Spartans must have seemed irrelevant. They were fighting more than three hundred men. They were fighting a legend, and for three miraculous days the legend prevailed.

For centuries many leaders have realised that history can be a much more powerful weapon than any bunker busting bomb; Julius Caesar, Napoleon and Hitler to name but three. If you convince a man that he is a part of a glorious history, he will punch way beyond his weight. Do it right, and men can achieve what on paper seems impossible. Like the Spartans at Thermopylae. Like the Legionaire Paratroopers at Dien Bien Phu. Like the British squares on the fields of Waterloo.

Armies have learned well over the centuries how to harness the power of history. Instinctively we human beings will always be pack animals. Young gang members prefer silence and prison to breaking the code of the pack. Rival football fans knock ten bells out of each other for the sake of the scarf around their necks. All kinds of different human gangs rely on myth and ceremony and history to bind in members. Friedrich Nietzsche wrote at length in his own rather crazy way about how to turn a man into a superman and tragically Hitler got the book out of the library and the rest was history.

Once you take a step back, it is possible to see that the template for achieving this kind ultimate gang has changed little from the Spartans to Napoleon's Imperial Guards to Hitler's Grossdeutchland Division to the

French Foreign Legion. You take a man, and then you knock ten bells out of him for several months whilst all the while telling him that he is becoming part of something that is unique. Special. Elite. Historic. Unbroken and unbreakable. You bind him in with history and tradition and legend. You make him feel that he has become a part of something that has been hundreds of years in the making. And if you do your job right, then he will soon feel that he has become a part of something that that is extraordinary. An ultimate gang that only a privileged few can ever be a part of.

Of course there is no argument whatsoever that this kind of mentality has huge benefits on the battlefield. Wellington would have had no chance if his squares hadn't held firm. Time and again the British army has dug itself out of seemingly bottomless holes as a result of a dogged refusal to accept the odds. For hundreds of years our squares have never broken and as a result we have often managed to find victory from the gaping jaws of defeat: Rorke's Drift, the miracle on the Marne, Dunkirk, Goose Green.... The list is a long one.

And yet sometimes when huge bodies of men are irrevocably steeped in the legend and history of their units, the result can be very different and quite frankly desperate. We look back and shake our heads with the benefit of hindsight and wonder to ourselves why on earth did they do that? What on earth got into them? A third of a million Germans died defending Berlin from the advancing Red Army when defeat was a given. Why on earth did they do that? What possessed the Foreign Legionaires at Dien Bien Phu to refuse to surrender even when they were down to holding a bomb churned patch of ground little bigger than a couple of football pitches?

At its best, the 'square mentality' can achieve miracles in the face of impossible odds. At its worst it drives men to needless death by fighting on when it is plainly futile. Obviously this isn't a thing that an army can ever consider. An army has to fight so long as there is a chance of success and it has to train its men accordingly. Armies that break and run are little use to anyone. The 'square mentality' has been with us since the dawn of time and no doubt it will be around as long as men walk on top of this earth.

We are very good at glorying in the times when the squares remain firm against all odds. What a film 'Zulu' was! Sadly, I wonder if we are quite as good at understanding the consequences that those who have the 'square mentality' drilled into them have to deal with. When a man has drilled and drilled and drilled never, ever to show a chink of weakness, it is a very hard habit for him to shake. In fact it can often be impossible. The men who are trained to form up into squares and face down the enemy learn to bury any weakness very, very deep. They hide it away. They lock it down behind fifteen foot high walls. And when they hang up their uniforms and check in their kit for the final time, they are still deeply programmed to bottle up any hint of weakness. To show it would mean losing something precious. To show it would jeopardise their place in the line. And that is a price that few are willing to pay and who can blame them.

I asked Don to guess how many of the men he served with during his fourteen years in uniform had found normal life hard to deal with once they left the army. How many had nightmares? How many had hit the slippery slope? He answered with an air of embarrassment, whilst promising that he wasn't being alarmist. In his opinion the figure was fifty percent. If Don was willing to say fifty percent, my gut feeling is that it is probably nearer seventy five. He told me about a sergeant major who had rotated between his battalion and the SAS throughout the 70's. The man was an alpha soldier in every way, most particularly in his shooting prowess. And now? Now he is a tramp eking out an existence on the streets of Surrey. He is one of those bleak guys standing in the rain selling the Big Issue to raise the cash for the next carrier bag of super lager. An awful lot must have gone wrong with his life since he left the army, but it seems a fair bet that he will never have shown the eyes of the world any weakness. Not once. Not ever. He might have lost everything and be out there standing in the rain, but his core pride is no doubt still in one piece. Maybe if he had been able to ask somebody for some help things might have worked out differently. But to have asked for help would have cost him more than he was willing to pay. Just like the Legionaires who preferred death to surrender at Dien Bien Phu. To most of us who have never been trained to form up into a square, this is something that is impossible to conceive. We live in a society where millions attend sessions with shrinks and agony aunts ply their trade in magazines and men are encouraged to show their emotions. This is a world that the likes of Don have never come close to joining. To do so would go against everything they have ever been taught.

To show weakness would put the whole square in jeopardy. It would mean shame and self disgust. And the quiet disdain not only of their comrades, but also of all the men who manned the squares of history. Is this price they are willing to pay? No chance. So instead they face forward and suffer their demons in silence.

For years and years and years.

For Don it was thirty five years.

Half a lifetime.

Men take the King's shilling and join up for all kinds of reasons. For Don it was down to a tedious bus journey. In 1968 his dad received a promotion which meant that the family moved fifteen miles up the road. For twenty year old Don, this meant a bus journey to and from work. And he hated it. It drove him mad. It convinced him that he needed a change. And so he decided to join the army.

His uncle had been in the Scots Guards and so there was a family tradition to follow. (Another relative had served on HMS Hood in the Second World War and had missed his ship sailing when the train returning him back from leave had been delayed. As it turned out, this was a hugely lucky break as the Hood sailed away to meet its nemesis care of the Bismarck.)

For the first time in his life Don found himself on a train which carried him south to the Guards barracks in Purbright, Surrey. He asked a bus driver to drop him off when they got to the gates. The driver forgot all about it, which meant that when Don eventually found a set of gates, they were the wrong ones. He had already been issued a full set of kit by the Royal Engineers before he realised he was in the wrong place.

Basic training was endless and murderous and every morning he woke up hoping to find himself back in his own bedroom at home. Of course he never did. Instead he finished his four months and was allowed to wear his uncle's cap badge on the day he passed out.

Though basic training had been very hard, there had been nothing about it that Don hadn't expected. He knew that being a soldier meant being fit, disciplined, skilled and willing to follow orders without hesitation. His uncle had given him plenty of clues as to what it meant to be a Guardsman. His basic training put flesh on the bones. History and tradition. Tradition and history. A history that stretched all the way back to 1642. Battle honours and medals from all corners of the earth. Five Victoria Crosses in the First World War alone. And towering above almost everything else, there was the almost impossibly heroic defence of the farm at Hougoumont which in the opinion of Wellington had turned the battle of Waterloo and the course of history. It all meant that he was more than a mere infantry soldier. He was a part of three hundred and twenty six years of history. And with that came a responsibility to always stand firm. To never show weakenss. To take anything that was thrown at him.

A boat and three hours on the road took him to his first posting with the Battalion. Munster. Germany. NATO. Cold War. In theory the greatest battle of them all to be prepared for. In practice, a whole lot of hanging around. When the new guys arrived at the camp they were given a list of appointments for the next day and then shown to their quarters. Being fresh out of basic training meant that all their kit was in apple pie order and needed little sorting. The evening was their own, and so they made their way to the camp bar.

The camp madhouse.

Don had never seen anything quite like it. Guys were not just drunk. They were utterly slaughtered. The scene that he walked into was unlike anything he had ever witnessed. The room was like a tip. Sometimes guys managed to stagger to the toilets to unload the gallons of extra strong and ultra cheap Heineken they had necked. Sometimes they were incapable of making the trip and pissed against the wall instead. Nobody seemed to notice. It was no big deal. It was obviously just normal. Guys were up on the tables with their trousers around their ankles and burning lengths of toilet roll rammed up their backsides. Firedancing.

The drinking was on an industrial scale. All part of the ethos. The tradition. Part of the 326 years. They had probably firedanced in the smoking ruins of Hougoumont.

Here was a tradition that Don had no problem becoming a part of. For the next fourteen years he became one of the Battalion's hardest drinkers. Not a problem. You fought hard, you drank hard. Why not? It was how it was. How it had always been. And if anyone screwed up whilst they were hammered, then his mates would cover for him. Obviously they did.

Next stop London. Bearskin strapped tight outside the gates of Buckingham Palace. Two hours at a time in the rain and the sun and the snow. Staring straight ahead, oblivious to the constant stream of tourists and their cameras. Click, click. Daddy can you take one of me standing next to him? Daddy do you think he's hot in that big hat? Daddy, do you think he's breathing. Eyes front. Never move. Not a twitch. Like on the walls of Hougoumont. Part of the history. Part of the 326 years. And a after the two hours it would be the bar and drinking and drinking and drinking.

But then things became unexpected. All of a sudden black and white televisions carried extra-ordinary images from Ulster. Belfast had gone berserk. It looked like a city at war. Houses blazed. Policemen waded into baying crowds with crashing batons. There was shooting on the streets. The experts were worried that the whole place was sinking into anarchy. Could the Royal Ulster Constabulary hold the line? Apparently not. Could the Ulster Defence Regiment hold the line? Nah. James Callaghan the Home Secretary flew out and took a look and flew back. It was time for Plan B.

With hindsight, what happened next was ominous. The battalion was shipped across the water and straight up Lagan Loch into the centre of burning Belfast. They didn't use P&O or Stena Line. They sailed on a troop carrier called the Sir Galahad. The next time Don would see the Sir Galahad would be thirteen years later as it billowed flames and black smoke in Bluff Cove. They were trucked 14 miles to the west of the city to put up their tents on an old RAF station. It was a reasonable enough choice. It was MOD land that was doing nothing; tucked out of the way, but still within easy reach of where the streets were burning and barricaded. It went by the name of Long Kesh. A couple of years later the government used the same ground to erect wire cages around the Nissan huts as part of their new internment policy. Twelve years later the same ground was used to build the iconic H Blocks of HMP Maze where twelve men starved themselves to death as the world looked on.

Don's first experience of being a soldier on active service was by no means a terrible one. For a start it didn't last all that long. Just over a month. By and large the people of Belfast were delighted to see the Scots Guards. They brought a semblance of order to the sectarian lunacy that had swept the Province. The lads carried live weapons but never discharged them. More to the point, nobody discharged any live weapons in their direction. His first taste of Northern Ireland was all about road blocks and riot duty and neither was a problem. Back in the sixties, riot duty was something that any British soldier was well trained to carry out. For twenty years Britain had been easing itself out of its Empire and there had been plenty of riots to deal with along the way from Calcutta to Jerusalem to Aden. Riots were not a problem. Not when you were young and fit and up for it.

Four weeks and it was a case of job done and back to getting his photo taken outside the gates of the Palace. Soldiering was a fine thing indeed.

In 1971 the Battalion returned to Ulster and the world turned dark. The Republican community had been steadily turning against the soldiers. It had been OK at first when they had come in to calm things down. But more and more they were considered unwelcome. Especially the Scottish regiments who were seen to be hand in glove with the Ulster Loyalists. The IRA were no mugs at the history game themselves. It didn't take all that very long for them to dig out the facts from the Battalion's early days. In 1641 the local Irish had risen up to try and throw the new Scottish settlers into the Irish Sea. Well London decided that this wouldn't do at all. A lesson needed to be taught. King Charles took a ride down to his Parliament to ask for the cash to raise a force of 1500 men to be 'led into our royal realm of Ireland'. Parliament was all for the idea and gladly wrote out the cheque. The 1500 men were duly raised and shipped over the water and so the Scots Guards were born.

So there was some history there and few people in the world do history better than the Irish. This time the Battalion was split up and quartered across the city. And wherever they were based, they flew their flag. Which of course was the Lion Rampant. As in a red rag to a bull. And for the first time the Irish Republicans started shooting at British Army soldiers. Shooting and killing. Belfast went beyond the riot stage and became a war zone.

It was the very worst kind of soldiering. In both theory and practice, the Battalion was now in a war zone. Hostile territory. In harm's way. And yet nothing was simple. The surroundings were disconcertingly familiar. This was not a sun bleached city of white houses somewhere in Arabia. Instead, Belfast was just like any other northern British town of terraced streets and constant rain. The tins of beans on the shelves of the corner shops were the same brand as they were in similar shops at home. The currency was the pound, the language was English, and the Queen's head was on the postage stamps. There were rusty looking Ford Cortinas on the streets and people watched Morecambe and Wise on a Saturday night. So it's good night from me, and it's good night from him…

Fourteen hundred ninety nine thousand and seven hundred of those who lived in Ulster were regulation British citizens and they were to be treated accordingly. About three hundred were armed terrorists who were ready, willing and sometimes able to shoot British soldiers.

It wasn't a case of see a bad guy and fire. That wasn't how things were to done. Every squaddie was issued with a yellow card explaining the exact procedure that should be followed in the event of a player in a black balaclava jumping out of a doorway with his Armalite at the ready. And if that exact procedure wasn't followed to the letter, the very same British squaddie could find himself up in front of a Crown Court judge facing murder charges.

It would take another quarter of a century for the British Army to work out how to take on the IRA and win. In 1971 everyone was right at the beginning of the learning curve and it didn't take very long for soldiers to start paying the ultimate price. The dismal hate filled streets of Belfast offered none of the clear cut clarity of the walls of Hougoumont. There was no massed enemy to face down. Instead there were women in headscarves and prams. Teenagers in frayed tank tops flicking V signs. Shop windows carrying adverts for Persil and Heinz and Kleenex.

A riot somewhere across the city. The radio calls in help. More numbers needed. Move, move. The line is too thin. Too few shields in the line. Baying voices. The air filled with missiles. Lumps of concrete. Half bricks. Bottles. Petrol bombs. Chaos. Chaos. Thunderous sound. Screaming voices. Hatred so thick you can touch it. Stiffen the line. Re-inforce. Remember what it says on the card. Hold your nerve. Don't lose your rag. Swear at the bastards if you like. Smack your baton into your shield if you like. But for Christ's sake don't fire.

Snatch squads. The line of shields opens and teams burst out to grab the gobby ones and drag them back behind the line. In and out. Fast and furious. Maximum aggression. Smack the shields hard.

Shit.

A snatch squad in trouble. Not fast enough. Engulfed. Swallowed up. Trying to get back to the line. Bottles and bricks and screaming abuse. Shit. For Christ's sake don't fire. Remember to follow the card. One of them back now. Two of them back now.

Oh shit.

One still out there. Down on the floor. Down with the broken glass and the half bricks. For Christ's sake don't fire. Follow what it says on the card.

Oh shit.

Women. Lots of women. They've got their shoes off. Stiletto shoes.

Hammering and hammering and hammering. Hammering the man on the ground with stiletto shoes. Screaming hate. Like a pack of wild dogs. For Christ's sake don't shoot! Follow the card! Go,go, go!!!!! A charging line of screaming, swearing shields. Enraged. Driving the mob back down the street. Women running gimp in only one shoe. Carrying stiletto shoes dripping blood.

A body on the ground.

A body as red and lifeless as meat on the slab.

Don's company commander decided that it would be best to drive the lads hard. He instigated a harsh routine to keep their minds focused on the job in hand. It was something he had made up himself. Something to get him noticed. Something to accelerate his progress up the ladder. Eight hours foot patrol. Eight hours mobile patrol in Land Rovers or Saracens. Eight hours guard duty. Twenty four hours at a time. No breaks. Then back to base for a quick scoff and what sleep as could be had. Eight hours to eat and wash and arrange kit and sleep. And then another twenty four hours. Soon they were all mind numbingly tired and completely pissed off. No other company was on this kind of regime. But their commander knew best. They could take it. Of course they could. They were Guardsmen. It would keep them focused. Sharp. Honed. No need to give them any time to think. What good would that do? Better to work them. Drive them.

Patrolling. Always patrolling. Women and prams. Old boys walking dogs. Kids with footballs. Cobbled streets. Washing on the line. Women gossiping in the doorways. Buses. Teenagers mouthing off. And every corner is a threat. Every upstairs window is a threat. There is the sound of shooting from across the city somewhere. The radio squawks news of a man down. The sound of Radio One comes through the window of passing vans.

Boom.

What the hell? Where the hell? News from the net. Bomb in the command post. Not in it. Next door to it. A bloody butchers shop. Two pounds of pork chops love? Here you go. Your man well is he…

A bloody butchers shop next door.

A bomb that has flattened the wall between the shop and the post. Get there. Go,go,go!! Anyone in there? Christ. Shit. The cook. Where is the cook? Christ. Shit. Dig for Christ's sake.

A crowd on the street now. Nosy. Some smiling. Smug. Pleased. Watching the frantic soldiers dragging away at bricks and concrete. Digging for the cook who was inside when the bomb in the butcher's shop blew. Keep your cool. Ignore them. Just dig. For Christ's sake don't fire.

I think I can feel something…..

Is he moving…..

Is he breathing….

Shit.

Oh Christ.

Smug faces as the wrecked body of the cook is pulled clear. Covered over and driven away. Just a bloody cook. For Christ's sake don't fire.

It's not like the walls of Hougoumont.

It's just another street in Belfast.

A dead cook.

A smoking hole where there was once a butcher's chop.

Pound of sausages love?

Follow the card.

For Christ's sake don't fire.

Down time.

Just eight hours. Then back to the streets. Tired, tired, tired. Corridors and doors. Which way were the showers? Tired, tired, tired. What is going on in there? What the hell…

Shit.

Christ.

A young woman tied to a chair, her face a mask of blood….

A plain clothes copper pistol whipping her like a man possessed.

What the hell do you think you're doing…..

Just piss off. Nothing to do with you. Get the hell out.

Go get your shower.

Twenty four hours on. Eight hours off. On and on it went. On twelve occasions they came under fire. Sometimes they returned fire. Maybe they hit. Maybe they didn't. When there had been a contact the Military Police would arrive at the base to ask their questions. To take notes. To make sure that the rules on the card had been followed properly. To the letter. Maybe this took an hour. Maybe two hours. However long it took, it came out of the eight hours set aside for washing and eating and sleeping and knocking back the two cans that were allowed after each twenty four hour shift out on the streets. And so after the questions there might have only been five hours to wash and eat and sleep. Or four. Not that it mattered. They were Guardsmen after all. They didn't need sleep or time to think. They were kept busy. Kept out there on those wet cobbled streets. Twenty four on and eight off. Unless the eight was five.

Patrolling and patrolling and patrolling. Persil whiter than white in the shop windows. Kleenex for men in the shop windows. Beanz Meanz Heinz in the shop windows. Twenty four on and eight off. Remember to follow the card.

Move and cover. Cross. Wait. Radio in. Move and cover. Parked cars and litter bins. Front steps. Broken paving stones. Soldiers on both pavements. Crouching. Sighting down their weapons. Cover and move. Every high widow a danger. Every street corner a danger.

Man crossing.

Crouch and cover.

Pop pop.

Shit.

Oh Christ.

Man down. In the road.

Shit.

Who?

It's the new lad. Poor sod.

Only just 17 and fresh across the water from his basic.

Shit.

Got to get him.

Pop pop.

Thump thump.

Oh Christ.

Can't get to him. Only five feet but it might as well be five miles.

Exposed. Scared. Screaming. Down.

On the floor. On the tarmac. In the grime. Just a bloody kid. Just bloody seventeen.

Pop pop.

Thump thump.

Oh you bastards!

You lousy cowardly bastards. You've already hit him. He's down for Christ's sake. Isn't that enough? Just a kid.

Pop pop.

Thump thump.

Bastards.

Bastards bastards bastards,

And where are they? Just give me a glimpse. A face. A target. Something to drop. But this isn't the walls of Hougoumont. This is a street in Belfast. And there are adverts for Persil whiter than white in the shop windows. And Kleenex for men. And Beanz Meanz Heinz. And the kid isn't moving any more. He'll never move again. He's gone. Glassy eyes staring up into the grey sky. And through it.

Radio. Contact over. Load him up. Move him out. Only seventeen.

Bastards,

Seven times they shot him.

Pop pop pop pop pop pop pop

Thump thump thump thump thump thump thump

One two three four five six seven

Bastards.

But there is no room for any of that. No time to think about it. No room in the head for the lad who is only seventeen.

Cover and move. Move and cover. Persil whiter than white. Beanz Means Heinz. Kleenex for men.

Eight hours foot patrol.

Eight hours mobile.

Eight hours on guard.

Military police. How many rounds did you discharge? Did you abide by the instructions on the card?

And nobody talks about him. Nobody even mentions him. He's gone now. That is all there is. Too tired. Too numb. Eat. Wash. Sleep. And then eight hours foot patrol. Eight hours mobile. Eight hours guard. Eat. Wash. Sleep.

He's gone.

Fill the line with someone else. Eyes forward. Calm. No weakness.

A British square never breaks.

But this isn't the walls of Hougoumont.

This is Belfast 1971.
Persil whiter than white
Kleenex for men.
Beanz Meanz Heinz.
And it's goodnight from me and goodnight from him…
Pound of sausages love….
Only seventeen.
One two three four five six seven.
Bastards.

For two years Don was OK with it. He followed the routines and when the day was done he hit the bar hard. The images of 1971 were all locked away. Out of sight was out of mind. He was a Guardsman. Bad stuff happened. It was all part and parcel. Par for the course. Being a Guardsman meant getting the head down and getting on with it. You didn't moan about it. You didn't fret about what might have been. Bad stuff happened and that was that. It wasn't a thing that any of them would talk about. Sometimes things would be very quiet. Sombre. When a man had been lost. But it was never up for discussion. That wasn't how things were done.

But sometimes cupboards refuse to stay closed no matter how hard you try to lock them tight. If you put a great big bloke behind a thin door, he's bound to kick it off the hinges at some stage. Lock or no lock. And then all of sudden he is right there in the room with you. Huge. Raging. Filling all the space. Red faced and breathing stinking breath in your face. Oh you can ask him nicely to go away please. To get back into the cupboard. To step back. To stop breathing his foul breath in your face.

Well you can ask.
And you and beg and plead and try to reason with him.
But he's not that kind of bloke.
He's there in your face and he's not about to go anywhere fast.

And so it was that in 1973 the nightmares started. Sometimes they would only come every now and then. Sometimes it would be every night. Always back to 1971. Night after night taking him back to the wet streets where every first floor window carried the threat of death.

One two three four five six seven
Pop pop pop pop pop pop pop

Thump thump thump thump thump thump thump.

Only five feet away.

Always five feet away.

Down hard on that Belfast tarmac.

Locked in time at the age of seventeen.

Seventeen forever and ever.

Night after night Don would be there just five feet away as the high velocity bullets thumped into the doomed boy.

One after another.

Until the boy's screams died away and his eyes turned to glass and stared up into the grey skies above.

And night after night Don could never do anything to stop it. It was only ever five feet, but it might as well have been five miles. And there was never a night when the bastards were willing to settle for one hit. It always had to be seven.

On other nights he was once again digging at the collapsed walls of the base next door to the butcher's shop, but he was never in time.

On other nights he was back behind his shield watching the rise and fall of the stiletto heels.

And morning after morning he would wake up feeling drained and bled dry. But he never said anything. Had he said anything, he would have been an outcast. They would have moved him from the line. There was no room for men who showed weakness. He was a Guardsman. End of story.

So he bottled it all up. And he hit the bottle. And got his head down. And got on with it.

Years passed and still the nightmares came. Except with each tour in Ulster there were new images. New memories. New fuel for the fire that burned away in his head night after night.

1975

Another year, another tour.

This time they are out of Belfast. A small northern town of terraced streets and estates with flags and kerbstones painted according to different sides of the coin. On one side there are Union flags and red white and blue. On the other side it is the Irish tricolour and green, white and gold. Colours of difference. Colours of hatred. Seven hundred years worth.

They are based in a police station. Corrugated iron walls and watch towers on the corners. Just a slow sort of day. Traffic noise from the road outside. Nothing much doing. Time to be killed. Down time.....

Cruummppp…

Incoming. Mortar fire.

Crummppppppp….

Closer. Much closer. Ranging in.

Crummppppppppppp!!!!!

Shit.

Christ.

Way closer. The next one will be the one. Maybe the last one. Everyone is frantic but there is nothing to be done. No time. No options.

Shit.

Crummmppppp.

Much further away. What the hell? The players must have lost the plot. Everyone looks at each other. Everyone has been counting down their last seconds. Then nothing.

What the hell?

Orders. Move, move. Get out. Hit the streets. Locate and find.

A patrol bomb-bursts through the police station gates and hits the streets with thumping boots.

Move, move.

Locate and find.

And they find it. The flat bed truck where the mortar fire had come from. And now all is clear. The last bomb has gone off in the faces of the players. The one that would have been the killer has never made it out of the tube. It seems like there has been two of them. Hard to tell. There's not a lot left. Bits here. Bits there.

Christ.

The senior guys get their heads together and make a decision. There are a couple of young lads in the company fresh out of basic. It's time for them to learn how things are. The new lads are ordered up in into the truck. To look at what is left. To face the reality. To confront the horror. One throws his guts up, but they manage to take it. Welcome to the world of the Guardsman. Hey guys, it wasn't so pretty after Hougoumont either.

And at the time it seems like the right thing to do. And maybe it is the right thing to do. But later in the dark hours of the night, the dreams that come into Don's head suggest otherwise.

Over and over and over.

And still he never said a thing. Never mentioned it to a single soul. He did what he was trained to do. He took it in his stride. He faced front. He waited for the order to fire. And the square never broke.

The 70's became the 80's and little changed. Don suffered his nightmares and kept them to himself. By now he had a reputation as being one of the harder drinkers. The alcohol often put him on the wrong side of authority much like a teenager out and about on late night weekend streets. Fines paid. Time served. He took it in his stride. Accepted the punishment when it came. For years he looked to the booze to solve the problem of the nightmares. To help him to hide away from all the images that refused to leave him alone. Instead, the drink became a problem in itself, much like the kind of pal who constantly gets into bother and drags you along with them.

1982.

Journey's end. The journey was a twelve thousand mile cruise south to some islands that nobody had ever heard of in 1981. The Falklands. Don chuckles at the memory. He had never in his wildest dreams ever thought he would take a long cruise on the QE2. It would have maybe been one of those 'when I win the Lottery' thoughts. Not that there was a Lottery to win in 1982. And when the QE2 dropped anchor, it wasn't by some sun kissed white beach in the Caribbean.

Fat chance.

Instead it was the rough grass and rocks of Bluff Cove. An instead of mooring up next to a line of millionaire yachts, the QE2 came to halt next to the Sir Galahad and scenes from the bottom levels of hell. The battalion came under fire the minute they got ashore. Casualties taken. No time to consider it.

Move, move.

Find cover.

Group up.

Move, move.

Flames and towering black smoke and the screaming of low flying jets.

Group up and get going.

It is 1982 and the Battalion has gone back to the Low Tech days of the Middle Ages. Ground to cover and no vehicles available.

So it's Shanks's pony.

Get your packs on and walk lads.

And walk and walk and walk.

Wet boots and soft lousy ground and cold as hell.

Blisters and chafed everything. Twelve thousand miles to the north the tabloids are calling it yomping.

Yomp and yomp and yomp and they keep going, pushed on by the legend of Hougoumont and all those other times Guardsmen had kept going for 340 years.

Until on the horizon there is a hill. A windswept moor. The kind of hill that could be found more or less anywhere in Scotland. They say it's called Tumbledown. They say that Port Stanley is just a few miles on the other side. They say the Argies are on the top.

A pause. Some time to regroup. The Welsh Guards have already had a pop at it and got knocked back. Now it's time for the Jocks to have a crack.

Any air cover? No. What about artillery support? Maybe. Tell you what lads. Get up there at night. Use the darkness.

Shit.

And thankfully the Argentinian troops at the top are mostly just kids. Conscripts. Half starved and frozen and deserted by their officers. Don makes the top and his company is unscathed.

How would it have been if there had been a unit of well armed, well led professional soldiers on the top of that hill? Don't go there. Don't even go close. Just get on with it. Face front.

They can see Port Stanley now. Just a tin pot sort of place by the sea. What the hell is the point? How many Argies are there down there? No idea. How well armed are they? No idea.

So what are we going to do then?

Attack.

Shit.

So when are they bringing us more ammo then?

They aren't. There's no ammo left. It all went down with the Sir Galahad.

Shit.

But hang on a minute, we've only got six rounds each.

Well it will have to do. Fix your bayonets. It'll all be fine. You're Guardsmen.

Are you seriously telling us to assault that place down there with six rounds each?

Yup. Don't forget to fix your bayonets.

How would it have been if the Argentinians had chosen to fight rather than surrender? How would it have been with only six rounds and a bayonet?

The Brass have bet the farm on pair of fives. A complete bluff and now they are glowing with their brilliance.

But how would it have been for the poor buggers with six rounds each and a bayonet if the big gamble hadn't come off?

Don was totally pissed off with all of it. Being a soldier was one thing. Being cannon fodder was another thing altogether. After fourteen years and a million nightmares he felt that the army had shown some true colours. They had been willing to gamble his life and the life of every one of the Guardsmen who had advanced down from the mountain with six rounds and a bayonet. The fact that the gamble had paid off was irrelevant. It was the fact that his life had been considered to be so completely expendable that ate into Don like a cancer.

The Battalion returned to its duties in Hong Kong and Don dealt with things as he always dealt with things. He stayed drunk for a month. Really drunk. Raging drunk. And at the end of the month, he decided that he was done with it all.

It was time to get out. He couldn't get his head around the way the Brass had been willing to gamble their lives so recklessly. And for what? Oil? Pride? Thatcher keeping the keys to Number 10? A last pathetic attempt to hang onto a last pathetic piece of Empire? Don had no idea why. All he knew was that it all seemed to him to stink like a pile of rotting fish.

And so he filled in the forms and signed on the dotted lines and was given a leaving date.

Any chance of a flight home sir? Are you kidding? We'll put you on one in a few months time. We don't do favours to men who want to leave.

He took the bus into Kowloon and bought himself a ticket.

He packed and then on his leaving day a message came down from the CO. Since Don wasn't leaving until 3pm, there was plenty of time for him to renew his BFT. Basic Fitness test. So many miles in so many minutes. Full pack? Of course full pack. Do it in the heat and humidity Don. Just so you know what we think Don.

Basic Fitness Test renewal. A month earlier he had yomped for nine days and now they wanted him to renew his BFT. He told them to bugger off.

And that was that.

Fourteen years all they could think of by way of a thanks for your efforts Don was to tell him to renew his BFT.

He got on the plane and returned home to a civilian life.

Normality.

Except it never was quite normal. Not really.

Things were normal enough on the surface. Jobs. Houses. Marriage. There were blips, usually caused by the drinking. A licence lost. Bother here and there. But nothing all that dramatic. In some ways, Don felt he was one of the luckier ones. There were others he had served with who had hit the bricks completely and become lost souls. Outcasts in rags, drowning in drink, bleary eyes fixed on places and things nobody else could see. He wasn't down there.

So maybe things were OK.

Or maybe not.

And the years ticked by. The nineties. The noughties. Tick,tick,tick.

Mobile phones the size of bricks appeared and then they slowly got smaller and smaller.

The Cold War ended with a crash of Berlin concrete on a cold November night.

The Millenium came and went and the world didn't end after all.

And a kind of peace broke out on the mean streets of Belfast where once there had only been hate.

Each day saw the world move on. But Don's nights remained a time warp. Sleep still took him back to those same desperate days.

Persil whiter than white.

Kleenex for men.

Beanz Meanz Heinz.

And it's good night from me, and it's goodnight from him.

That's neat, that's neat, that's neat, I really love those Tiger feet.....

Pop pop pop pop pop pop pop
Thump thump thump thump thump thump thump
Forever 1971
Forever seventeen,

And still the bastards would never leave the boy alone. Never settle on one hit being enough. Always seven.

One two three for five six seven.

And no matter how many times Don ran it and re-ran it through his dreams, there was never a time when he could do anything to stop them.

All he could so was drink.

And say nothing. Keep it all to himself. Face front. Maintain a calm expression. Man the line.

Because British squares never break.

But in the end there did come a breaking point.

It came on a bus. Ironic really. Don's journey had started as a result of a boring twenty minute bus journey. And now his turning point came on a bus. He was drunk. Very drunk. All afternoon in the pub drunk and making his way home. There was a couple in the seats in front. He didn't know them. They were just there. But when they got up to leave the bus, they took his shopping bags. What the hell!

An argument.

A fight.

The bus stopped and policemen were called and an arrest was made. Because it wasn't his shopping after all. It was their shopping all along. And Don had been so drunk that he had thought they were stealing his shopping and he had assaulted them.

When the clouds of alcohol slowly cleared, Don found himself living in a world of shame. The slippery slope that had caused him to first loose his footing way back in 1973 had finally delivered him to rock bottom. He had attacked a pair of complete strangers on a bus on a weekday afternoon. And for what? For nothing. He had acted like nothing better than a drunken lout.

And it was really, really hard to live with.

If you were to meet Don, you would soon see why. He's sixty now but he is still every inch the Guardsman who walked out of basic all those years ago. Smartly dressed and he still has that military bearing even though his back is all shot. It isn't all that hard to picture him in one of those squares of empire. He is absolutely not the kind of guy to attack strangers on a bus.

But that was exactly what he had done. And why? Because he was drunk. More than that, he had reached the stage when he was almost always drunk. Where he found it all but impossible to walk by the open doors of a pub.

He pleaded guilty of course and the Sheriff asked the criminal justice people to get some background reports together. A so it was that after thirty five years Don finally allowed the poison out.

He told.

Of a boy who came to him almost every night. A boy with pleading eyes. A boy with eyes that had lost their light that day on a Belfast street when one shot wasn't deemed to be enough.

Pop pop pop pop pop pop pop.

Thump thump thump thump thump thump thump

And he got lucky with his criminal justice worker. His man went the extra mile. He made enquiries and found out about Combat Stress and made the referral. And then he heard about a small place in Dumfries called the First Base Agency who had just started a project to help veterans.

And now?

Now things are better. Don had a week up at Hollybush House where they started the process of helping him to deal with the nightmares better. He has come to the conclusion that there is no point trying to hide from the dreams at the bottom of a bottle. Now he is learning techniques which help him to look his nightmares in the eye and hold his post. The people at Combat Stress are teaching how to stand in a different kind of square.

Now he keeps a drink diary and the number of units is falling fast. When we asked his criminal justice worker if he would like to come in to see us he was reluctant. Then we passed the message that we would be needing guys like him over the coming years to sit down and talk to the broken young soldiers who will be coming back from the killing fields of Helmand Province. At which point he came. Which of course says a lot about the guy.

And that is why he has agreed for his story to become a part of this book. It has taken Don thirty five years to reach out for some help. The irony is that once upon a time he would have called in help in the form of artillery or air support in less than thirty five seconds.

His message couldn't be clearer.

Asking for help doesn't mean the square will break.
So don't wait thirty five years to pick up the phone.
The number for Combat Stress is at the back of the book.
And the front.

## CHAPTER 3

## TREVOR

So, have you ever watched super hero movies? Well I guess that depends a bit on how old you are. Or maybe not? If you are in your mid twenties you will have grown up with the digitalised, hi-tech versions of Batman and Spiderman and Superman. However, I'm pushing fifty and yet I also grew up watching the same guys, although they looked and sounded a whole lot different on our old black and white tele rented from Granada! No matter, they still did their stuff. Add on a few years, and it would have been Dan Dare and the Lone Ranger and Buck Rogers. Hell, even Robin Hood. Errol Flynn wasn't anyone in particular. He was just Errol Flynn.

Although the size and scope of superhero movies has changed beyond all recognition, the basic storyline they follow never changes all that much. We usually find a put upon little guy who decides that enough is enough and so takes on the role of purging the world of the bad guys. When you take a step back, it can be a tad uncomfortable. I mean, is the law being followed to the letter here? Is this heroism or vigilantism? Ah come on, it's a cartoon for goodness sake.

And there tends to be another template which is followed to the letter. The small guy achieves super powers and takes on the forces of evil. The public love him to bits. Then some devious, crafty type, who tends to be rich and well connected, blackens our hero's name in the media and the public turn against him. Here is where things get a little pantomimish as the audience cannot quite believe how fickle the public are. 'How can you buy into all this!' we want to yell at the screen. Can't you see that you are being manipulated by the forces of evil? Thankfully, our hero tends to dig deep and come through against all odds and the public belatedly realise how wrong they have been not to have loved and trusted him all along.

I'm sure you get the picture.

At times we all have similar issues with our real life superheroes. When Para Colonel H Jones led his do or die, against the odds charge at Goose Green, we all loved our very own Supermen in maroon berets. And when the same Paras hacked their way to the top of Mount Longdon, a few weeks later, we loved them even more. The red tops went Para crazy. And why not? Here were the guys the nation could turn to when things got really, really bad. They were our Gladiators who would stand between us and the murderous hordes, no matter how lousy the odds.

And yet only ten years earlier, the red tops had painted a very different picture when the very same Paras shot down unarmed civilians on the streets of Londonderry.

When the SAS gave us prime time like we had never seen before on the roof of the Iranian Embassy, they became cult figures. When they took out three unarmed IRA men in Gilbralter a few years later, we were not so sure for a while.

These are of course questions of right and wrong that go back to the dawn of time. Is he a terrorist or a freedom fighter? French Resistance to a high tech army of occupation is good, whilst Afghani Resistance to a high tech army of occupation is evil. Is he a hero or a guy with major mental health problems who should be sectioned? Was it a magnificent victory worthy of a statue or was it a massacre? Is he an elite soldier to be given ultimate public respect or a cold blooded, trained assassin to be reviled? It is confusing. It always has been and it always will be.

Maybe the bottom line is that armies are expected to do whatever they have to do in order to win. Sometimes armies do terrible things and the public cheers them to the rafters. When we fire-bombed Dresden, there were few tears shed. Served them right was the prevailing mood. It was much the same when Enola Gay dropped Big Boy on Hiroshima. These were events that caused the civilian death toll to run into hundreds and hundreds of thousands, and yet it was deemed to be a more or less OK thing to do. But then when our soldiers killed 13 civilians on Bloody Sunday, the outrage was to last for thirty years and more. And still it goes on. The uranium tipped ordnance we dropped on Iraq in 1990 has killed off over half a million children with cancer, but nobody has ever appeared in court and the tabloids have never worked themselves into any kind of lather about it. And yet when a handful of soldiers lost the plot and beat Iraqi prisoners to death a few years later, there was national outrage and now guys are serving life sentences for murder.

Confusing, confusing, confusing.

And Trevor is confusing.

Very, very confusing!

Soon after I first met Trevor a few years ago, we fell into an ongoing row about what was basically copyright. In 2001 I wrote a book called 'The Cull'. It told the tale of a retired British Army Major who lost his son to a heroin overdose. Using the skills he had learned in Ireland, he took the fight to the drug dealers of Dumfries. But this time he had no rules and regulations to hold him back. The dealers were accustomed to the police being kept on a tight leash by the rigorous demands of the law which of course made the dealers feel safe and secure. As soon as the straight jacket of proper procedure and due process was taken away, the dealers suddenly became hugely vulnerable to the avenging father. It was all pure fiction of course, but lots of people liked it. I got umpteen e mails from coppers which basically said 'if only'.

A mate gave Trevor a copy of the book whilst he was serving in Iraq. 'The Cull' was set in Dumfries and Trev was from Dumfries, so it was only natural for his mate to pass on the copy. There ain't all that many books about Dumfries!

I had intended the book to be a down the line fiction with maybe a subtle warning of how Britain's spiralling drug crisis could lead to the kind of vigilantes that the public would approve of. In other words, the road to the same kind of guys ruling the roost as the ones who once wore brown shirts in Munich in the early 1920's.

Trev never saw it that way. Instead he saw it as a battle plan. A call to arms. Basically he saw it as a bloody good idea and once he left the Paras he was hell bent on turning the fictional story of Major Jack Sinclair into reality. He was quite convinced that I would be really pleased to have an ex Para using my book as an instruction manual to take down the bad guys. After all, there was no argument that the bad guys were truly bad and that they were peddling their poison to the kids of Dumfries on an industrial scale. He was quite pissed off with my reaction. I wittered on about the rule of law and how easily this kind of thing could lead to anarchy. Yeah, right! Like Trevor was ever about to buy into any of that! In the end the argument became clearly focused. I told him that it was my book, my idea, my story and he had no right to steal it without my permission. That would be a breach of copyright.

His view was that the idea was in the public domain which meant that it was OK for him get out there and do what needed to be done.

When you decide to become a writer you never imagine you'll find yourself in this kind of situation!

Trevor is a man who divides opinion every bit as much as the Parachute Regiment he served with such pride and distinction. This split is vividly described by the various written down reports that chart the course of Trev's life. For the first twenty years, there are plenty of pieces of official paper that tell the story of a boy forever in bother. Excluded from school, lifted by the law, kicking out at the walls of authority whenever he ran up against them. You can almost hear the voices of teachers and social workers and neighbours and policemen. Out of control. Out of line. Out of order. A bloody Ned! Nothing but trouble. Prison fodder. Get the picture? Sure you do. It's that all too common stereotype of modern Scottish youth.

Then there are a series of documents charting Trevor's four and a half year career with the Paras. Surely there must be a litany of offences and fines and stretches in the Brig? Wrong. Instead, the documents tell the story of a young soldier who never put a foot wrong. Check out the reference the Regiment gave him when he left. Were I a potential employer, I would rate it as Triple A Plus. Go on. Be honest. If you read that testimonial you'd give the lad a job wouldn't you? And why not?

But then there is a third set of documents that tell the story of the years since Trev hung up his maroon beret. You probably won't be all that very surprised to learn that these pieces of paper revert back those of Trev's youth. Out of control. Out of line. Out of order. A bloody Ned! Nothing but trouble. Prison fodder.

How can this be? Has he got a split personality? Or have the people who write the reports got a split personality? How can it be that he was able to excel in one of the toughest environments in the world and yet be deemed such a disgrace in the realm of normal life?

The more you get to know Trev, the more you get to wondering where the fault really lies in this confusion. Is the fault to be found in the man or in the way society judges him? You can probably guess that I tend to question society rather more than Trev. The police make no pretence about the fact that they would like to see him behind very thick bars for a very long time. In a way this is understandable. He is without doubt a formidable guy. You would definitely want him on your side in a scrap! The cops look at his Para training and they see him as a potential weapon of mass destruction. Trevor actually agrees with them to an extent. In a recent interview with Border TV he was brutally honest about the fact that if he didn't get some help in straightening out his brain that he might well kill someone. In these days of health and safety and duty of care to employees, many doors are closed in Trevor's face. Sorry, but we really can't allow you in the building I'm afraid sir. We've done a risk assessment you see. And we have assessed that you are a risk. In fact, in our opinion you are a trained killer. So we're very sorry, but you really can't come in.

At which point the door is closed quickly.

Nervously.

With a sigh of relief.

Oh we all loved the Paras when they stormed the enemy at Goose Green and Mount Longdon. Everybody loved them then. But they were at arms length then. A safe twelve thousand miles away. Maybe that is where we really want them. On the tele and in the papers, but not at the front door to the office asking for some help. A few days before the 2003 invasion of Iraq, 'The Sun' carried a picture of Trevor. The cameraman lined up the shot so that the reader could stare down the barrel of his gun into his eyes. Guess what the caption was. 'Deadly Paratrooper!' As in 'Deadly Paratrooper' = good. But as soon as the same young man leaves the Regiment, it doesn't take very long before that same handle is transformed into 'Deadly Paratrooper' = bad.

Confusing.

It reminds me of a line toward the end of 'Apocalypse Now' when a tortured Colonel Kurtz is recording his thoughts about the war his country is fighting. He is a few moments from being 'terminated with extreme prejudice' for the crime of being insane.

"We train young men to drop fire on people and yet their commanders won't allow them to write 'fuck' on their aeroplanes...... because .... It's obscene!"

It is a quote that is easily enough adapted for Trevor. We train a young man to be ultimately dangerous so that when the chips are down he will man the gates without fear or hesitation, but when he asks for some help we lock him out of the building ......because ...... he's trained to be ultimately dangerous.

So Trevor divides opinion. In a big way. Before getting on with the job of trying to tell his story, I will give you my opinion for what it is worth. I don't claim to be any kind of expert. I'm just a writer when all is said and done.

What I can say is that I don't think I have ever met anyone with such a burning sense of right and wrong. In a way Trevor is a man born out of time. Once upon a time his kind of almost religious fervour for striking down evil was deemed to be more than acceptable. Not any more it seems.

Of course we disagree on lots of things. I will always believe that the law is the only thing that keeps us from descending into becoming a Bosnia or a Rwanda. Of course it is flawed and of course it fails at times. But when all is said and done, it is all that we have got. Trev sees it rather differently. If he feels that the law is turning a blind eye to bad things happening, then he will ignore it and dive in. If you happen to be assaulting a pensioner whilst Trev is walking up the street, then God help you! I don't hold with his actions, but I wholeheartedly respect his motives. And yes it's confusing. When is a terrorist a freedom fighter? We never did manage to work that one out did we? Ever heard of a chap called Mandela…..?

Trevor's childhood was a long and lingering nightmare. His dad upped sticks and walked when he was five and he was soon replaced by a stepfather. Step parents have always tended to attract the label of 'wicked' in the world of children's fairytales, although it tends to be stepmothers who are the villains of the piece. More importantly, the abused child of the fairytale tends to find a way to walk into a happy ending. Well of course they do. We like to push real life domestic sad endings under the carpet and pretend they never happen. But it does happen of course. Day after day after day behind the locked front doors of modern Britain. Trevor's stepfather would have fitted easily into any storyline the Grimm Brothers ever worked on. Except they would have had to censor it. The levels of cold blooded brutality that Trev's stepfather reached would never have made the pages of any self respecting fairytale. Instead they would be more likely to be found in some obscure low budget Channel 4 film which is well received at the Cannes Festival but never makes it into the multiplex cinemas.

For whatever reason, the stepfather hated the stepson from the get go. No doubt he considered the five year old to be in the way, a nuisance, a pain. Unfortunately the man wasn't just your regular run of the mill bully. He was a champion of the bench press and loved nothing more than to try out his strength by beating his stepson.

On and on it went. Year after year. Every mistake or misdemeanour was punished by violence. And all the while the boy would watch TV and see how the world was supposed to be. Home was supposed to be the place where you were safe. Loved. Cared for. A sanctuary from the outside world. And when there was evil, there were always guys who would turn up to put things right, no matter how high the odds against success seemed to be. So it was that the young Trevor started to daydream about superheroes. Spiderman and Batman and Superman and James Bond. One day the front door would crash open and the blood would drain from his stepfather's face. Then it would be payback time as his tormentor would be felled in a flurry of Kung Fu moves.

Zap! Pow!!

The years passed and Trevor learnt that none of his pals were beaten like he was beaten. He had drawn the short straw. And that made him angry. Many, many years later psychiatrists feel that the young Trevor probably had some kind of hyperactivity. ADHD. He found it impossible to sit still in class. He couldn't seem to concentrate. His school work was lousy and the teachers never tired of telling him so. In a perfect world, concerned parents would have talked things through with concerned teachers and Trevor's problems would have been teased out and treated accordingly. But Trevor's world was a long, long way from being perfect. The school sent word that he was a problem kid and his stepfather beat the living daylights out of him

And all the while he got more and more and more angry.

And all the while he yearned for the day when one of those TV superheroes would turn out to right all the wrongs.

And the years passed and things started to escalate.

A teacher who hated him more than most asked him to return the pencil he had borrowed. She cupped her hands in front of her face ready to catch it. Trev sensed an opportunity for revenge and threw the pencil straight through the cupped hands and into her eye.

And all hell was let loose.

Reports were written. He was out of control they said. A wee thug. A horror. Get him out of sight and out of mind.

And so he was excluded from a place where life was a problem back to the place where life was a nightmare. And his stepfather beat him harder than he had ever beaten him before.

Once his time was served he was allowed back to school. By now he might as well have had a neon sign on his head saying 'Bad Boy Here!' Teachers gave him a wide berth. They weren't interested. The sooner the time came for him to leave the better as far as they were concerned. His mum and his stepfather never tired of telling him how useless he was. He would never amount to anything. He was thick. He was a loser. Prison fodder. He made them sick.

One of the school bullies couldn't resist tormenting the bad boy of the class. Why not? He was a foot and half taller than Trev and many pounds heavier. A farm boy, strong from lifting bales and mucking out. Day after day he picked away at Tev's mental scabs. Taunting. Mocking. Teasing.

Until one day Trev had his Spiderman moment by the bus stop and decided enough was enough. He worked it all out logically. He was used to being beaten by his stepfather. And his stepfather was a bench press champion and an adult. So if he wound up being beaten by the farmer boy bully, it would be as nothing when compared to what he was used to. And so he decided it was time to fight back. Like Batman. Like Superman. Like James Bond.

And he surprised himself.

Within seconds he had the bigger boy down on the pavement whilst the crowd cheered.

Scrap! Scrap! Scrap!

Then the red mist descended. All the years of being hammered came pouring out. He lost it. The time came to stop hitting. But Trev didn't stop. Just like his stepfather never stopped. And the watching crowd fell silent until adults arrived to drag him off.

This time the exclusion was much longer.

Nobody cared that the boy had been victimising Trev for months. Nobody cared that farmer boy was so much bigger. Why would they care? Trev was already labelled and packaged and filed away. Bad boy. Bad influence. Bad everything. Get him as far out of sight and out of mind as possible.

When he got back home, the mother of all beatings awaited him.

In the months that followed, his stepfather designed a new regime to torment his hated stepson. Trev would be put out of the house at eight in the morning and not allowed back in until late at night; rain or shine or snow. He was given garden tasks to complete. First he was ordered to move several tonnes of soil from the front garden to the back garden. Once that was done, he was given the task of removing three trees from the back garden. Not just the trunks and the branches, but the entire root system as well. And until the last trace of root was dug from the ground, he was to remain every bit as grounded himself. No time in the house. No time with his pals. Nothing.

For the months of his exclusion, Trev hacked away at those roots with a rusty hacksaw, a hammer and a pickaxe. And all the while his stepfather smirked at his efforts, knowing full well that the task was impossible. And when at last Trev would be allowed back inside the house late in the day, he would get a good beating to warm him up.

Once upon a time this kind of treatment was deemed to be character building. We Brits have always been rather good at it. One of the great pillars of our Empire was the public schools system. These were places where the boys who would grow up to rule Britain's vast dominions would be toughened up by a series of ritualistic beatings and beastings. When the boys became men, they would pay extortionate fees to join London clubs where they could exchange horror tales with each other over steamed pudding and custard. They would chuckle at the memory of how they had been abused and agree that it had been the making of them. Best thing that ever happened, what? And of course they sent their own sons to get a dose of the same medicine.

The brutality Trevor endured on a daily basis had a similar effect. He learnt how to take a beating. The long hours hacking at the tree roots built his strength. And all of a sudden, he had a goal. His stepfather sneered that he would never finish the task. Just like he never finished any task. Because he was useless. Because he was a waste of space. A loser. And so it was that Trevor learned stubbornness. He didn't care that the task was supposed to be impossible. Did Spiderman care? Did James Bond care? Did they give up when the going got tough?

Aye right.

And one day he finally took out the last root with a final almighty heave of his pickaxe. Then he walked inside and calmly informed his stepfather that he was getting changed and going out. Because the last root was gone. He turned his back on the livid face and went to his bedroom to get on some clean clothes.

And then the bedroom door opened just like he knew it would open and as he turned his step father felled him with a round house punch.

And once again the red mist descended. Trev managed to break the momentum of his fall and spring back forward. He put every last ounce of his body weight and anger and loathing into the kick he landed in his stepfather's face.

And the big man went down.

Hard.

On the floor of the bedroom with a nose pumping blood. Half conscious and confused.

And all hell let loose.

Policemen and social workers. And far too late the truth of years of vicious abuse came out and Trev was taken into care. But the carers knew that they would have to be careful. This was a problem kid. A bad boy. Dangerous and behind and angry. A health and safety risk. They got him well out of town to a unit in the depths of the countryside. Out of sight and out of mind. They wanted to keep a lid on until he was sixteen. Then he would be someone else's problem.

More walls.

More boundaries.

More people telling he was no good. A lost cause. People telling him that he would never amount to anything. How could he? He was a bad, bad boy who was useless in school. If he was really, really lucky, he might get a job on the bins. More likely he would wind up in jail.

At this point he started telling anyone willing to listen that one day he would join the army and prove them all wrong. And when they took the trouble to listen, they would laugh in his face. The army! Be serious. What would the army want with a lad like him? Stupid.

The more they told him it would never happen, the more he resolved to prove them wrong.

All of them.

Every last sneering one of them.

One day.

As he approached his sixteenth birthday he managed to persuade his carers to allow him to go to Newcastle to go and stay with his uncle. My oh my, they must have been diligent with their checks! Trev's uncle was due to hit the streets having served two years on remand for a brutal gangland killing which the police had failed to make stick, even though everyone in the city knew he had carried out the hit. Trev found himself in a flat with his uncle's girlfriend. It was more or less OK until the man himself was liberated. Trev only saw him for a day or two until his uncle upped sticks and moved across the city. Address unknown. He simply left his fifteen year old nephew in the flat. Well why the hell not? The boy was just a little shit. Stuff him. Who cared?

Nodody.

For days Trevor walked the streets of Newcastle getting hungrier and hungrier. And yet food was everywhere around him. In his face. In cafes and corner shops and market stalls. But he couldn't find away to steal it. Because always in his head were those superheroes. Would Spiderman nick a bag of crisps from the shelf? No. Would James Bond lift a bottle of milk from somebody's front step? Of course not.

So he went hungry,

And when he got really hungry he hitched back over the border to Dumfries.

Now came some better years.

He moved from place to place. Made pals. At last he was free from the locked down environments of home and care home. By now he had a 'rep'. Wannabe hard men wanted to claim his scalp, but it wasn't something that worried him greatly. When there was gossip at the post office counter or the bar of the pub or the checkout at the Spar shop, it tended to follow familiar lines. Bad boy. Nothing but trouble. Should be locked up. Complete nutter.

And still Trev told people that one day he would be a soldier. And once his back was turned, they would smirk and give each other knowing winks. Aye right. Dream on.

A tipping point arrived in the form of the BBC News. Kosovo was about to go the way of Bosnia. Evil Serbs in balaclavas were itching to start dispatching Muslims with sledgehammers. Here were guys who were as bad to the bone as any baddies in any Bond movie and Slobodan Milosevic was every inch a modern day Ernst Stavro Blofeld in his lair in Belgrade. The leaders of the free world had decided that enough was enough and it was high time to send in the good guys to sort it out. The Americans had ridden into town in all their high tech glory. One gum chewing Colonel in mirror sunglasses informed a delighted media contingent that they had come 'armed for bear'. And now the Brits were coming to the party.

Transport planes were disgorging soldiers who looked like pretty regular guys when compared to the action men style Americans. And then the doors on the back of one of the planes dropped down to the runway and Trevor found the path he wanted to walk.

For out of that plane strolled the Paras. For Trev they seemed completely different. Cooler than cool with their maroon berets and GIMPY machine guns held casually on their shoulders. They were calm and pro and exuded the air of men who were there to take care of business. Here were the guys from the right side. Here were the real life superheroes who he had once dreamed of coming to cave in the front door to beat the hell out of his stepfather. God help Milosevic and his murderous henchman. Payback time had arrived.

And Trev wanted to just like them. In fact he wanted to be one of them. He headed down to the recruitment office where as luck had it the sergeant was a Para himself. And for the first time in his life, Trev found an open door. Here were people who were not telling him he was useless. Of course you can join son. So long as you're fit enough. So long as you can hack it when the going gets tough. So long as you are stubborn enough to take all they will throw at you before you earn the right to wear that maroon beret.

Things looked fine. Better than fine. Finally he had found some direction. He filled in the papers and soon he was right on track. A couple of nights later he was in a night club when a stranger came along and smacked him in the face for no reason other than the fact that he was a local scalp to collect. Doormen piled in and a few minutes later Trev found himself bouncing his way to the bottom of the stairs where his assailant was waiting for a second go.

The wannabe tough guy duly piled into Trev who was very much aware that there were cameras filming the whole thing. The recruitment sergeant had made it very clear that a criminal record would screw everything up. And Trev wasn't about to let that happen. And so he took everything that his opponent had to give him, all the while telling him that he was going to be a Para and no way was he about to screw it up. After all, he was well enough used to taking a beating. His character had been well and truly built.

At last the tough guy got fed up and Trev wandered off bloodied but unbowed. A pal walked with him through the late night streets and asked if he was OK. Sure he was OK. He was going to be a Para. Fancy a joint? Yeah. Why not. A wall and a street light. Skin up and smoke.

Oops.

The night air was all of a sudden flashing blue. Would you like to come with us sir please? Could you empty you pockets please sir? We are going to have to confiscate this sir? I am arresting you on suspicion of being in possession of a Class C controlled substance sir, you have the right to remain silent….

The lab test confirmed their suspicions. In possession of a Class C drug. A fine. A record. The recruitment sergeant shook his head wearily. Silly bugger. You'll have to wait a year now.

But he was still on track. A year? So what? He could wait.

And he did wait, keeping his nose clean all the while until at last he took a train south to 'Stage One' training in Lichfield. And lo and behold, all that character building he had received care of his stepfather came good. The early weeks were all about pain. Lots and lots of pain. But Trev had come to know all about pain. And by now his stubborn streak was a mile deep. Sure the NCO's got in his face and gave him hell. But they did exactly the same to every one of guys. Here was a place where he had no history. For the first time in his life he was just one of the guys. Part of the team. And nobody told him that he was a waste of space. And the screamed abuse was no problem compared to the beatings of his childhood.

After eight months he was the proud owner of a maroon beret with a set of wings on the front. He had done what just about everyone in his life had told he would never do. He had achieved. He had endured. He had kept his nose clean. He had become a part of the elite.

And he had done it all on his own.

He became a part of 3 Para and everything was more or less as he had hoped it would be. There were a few downsides, but not many. Some of his fellow Paras fell a long way short of being the kind of guys he had watched marching down onto the runway in Kosovo. There were more racists than he was particularly comfortable with. Some adorned their walls with Swastika flags or posters of German paratroopers. It wasn't any great problem. He simply gave them a wide berth.

Platoon 'benders' were also a bit of a problem. Trev had never been much of a drinker and he hadn't any great wish to become one. However, anyone who failed to attend a platoon 'bender' would not be viewed with any kind of fondness. But again it was no great problem. He developed the knack of arriving late, having a couple of cans, and then slipping away unnoticed. All he was interested in was becoming the best Para he could be.

For two years things were tip top. He guarded the court in Omagh when the Real IRA bombers were unsuccessfully tried. He was part of the 3 Para detachment sent south to the Falklands for the twentieth anniversary. There were joint manoeuvres with US airborne troops at Fort Bragg where the highlight of the trip was catching a whole American platoon huddled around a campfire and wiping them out.

And then the newslines started to buzz with news that Bush and Blair had Saddam Hussein in their sights. It became more and more clear that a shooting war was on the cards and the Regiment was on permanent high alert. As far as Trevor was concerned, all was well in the garden. He had joined the guys in the maroon berets to go get the bad guys and they didn't come any worse than Saddam Hussein. Here was a Bond bad guy of the first order with his torture rooms and WMD.

The Regiment was moved out into the Kuwaiti desert where they trained for the big day. The ground was deemed to be too flat for a proper workout, so bulldozers where whistled up to create some hills for the Paras to run up and down loaded up with as much kit as they could carry. The days were all about getting in and out of the cumbersome spacesuits that promised protection from the most dastardly evilness Saddam had to throw at them. This was the time when a photographer grabbed a shot of a focused looking Trevor staring down the barrel of his gun. 'Deadly Paratrooper.' Fair enough he thought.

War was declared and Baghdad got first hand knowledge of what 'shock n'awe' was all about. Now the days became a whole lot more tense as the Scud missiles started to come across the border. One landed a few hundred metres from the Para's camp on the commandos. Suddenly it was the real deal.

Still no problem.

Trev hadn't joined up to learn to be plumber. He had joined up to go get the bad guys. It was his time.

And then they were taken through their battle orders and it became very clear that invading Iraq wasn't going to be another Arnhem or Goose Green or Mount Longdon. Their role was to get in there and protect the oil infrastructure.

And this was absolutely not how it was supposed to be.

Of course Trev had seen all the protests that had accompanied the build up to war. And he had heard all the doubting voices who said that the whole thing was about getting hold of Iraq's oil. But he had tuned it all out. It wasn't what he wanted to hear. The good guys wouldn't go in with all guns blazing to secure a few oil wells for a bunch of Texan billionaires. He preferred the Blair version. All the stuff about Britain being forty five minutes from getting hit by a selection of doomsday weaponry. All the stuff about how Saddam was Satan's representative on earth with his torture chambers and gas attacks.

But suddenly Trev found himself looking at the truth in black and white. Go over the border and secure the oil infrastructure. That was it. Pipes and pumps.

There were no last minute changes to the battle plans and when the great invasion was set rolling by London and Washington, 3 Para crossed the border and looked after the oil infrastructure. They dug trenches and every now and then they came under artillery fire.

A flat dusty boring place. Rusty old pipes. A sense of decay. Sometimes small clusters of villagers would wander along to have a nosey. More and more ragged looking Iraqi soldiers started to turn up with their hands up, looking beaten and unshaven and hungry. They were certainly a far cry from the gym-fit Norwegian types in black polo neck sweaters who made up the ranks of Ernst Stavro Blofeld's army.

Just frightened kids.

Frightened hungry kids wanting nothing more than to go home. Most of Trev's comrades found them to be figures of fun in their desperation. Pakis. Ragheads. Bastards.

And in the dark of the night, he would sit in his trench and hear the distant sound of the Ragheads being interrogated.

Screams.

Horrible piercing screams that reached deep into his head and took him all the way back to the days when his stepfather had beaten him in much the same way.

Guarding oil pumping equipment.

Sitting in trenches dug into a land of flat, dusty nothingness.

Listening to Paki jokes.

Listening to screaming in the still of the desert night.

It hadn't said any of this on the tin. They were supposed to be the ones to go get the bad guys. But it hadn't worked out that way. Instead it felt uncomfortably like they were the ones who were working for the bad guys. More to the point, they were behaving like bad guys. They were the ones causing the screaming in the night.

Weeks passed and hundreds of miles to the north the giant statue of Saddam crashed to the floor. Finally they got orders to move forward. By now the British had Basra surrounded. The streets of the Souk were too narrow for Challenger tanks. They were however quite wide enough for the Paras. They were to go in on foot. Carrying a hundred and twenty pounds of kit.

What the hell. At least it would mean some real war fighting against some real bad guys. However the Americans had different ideas. The day before 3 Para moved into town, American planes dropped a blizzard of leaflets on the population which gave out a simple message. The Paras are coming and they are seriously bad boys so if you have any sense you will lock your front door and keep your head down. In fact the leaflets mirrored the sentiments of The Sun: Deadly Paratrooper!

The good folk of Basra took heed of the message and locked their doors and kept their heads down. For Trev, the conquest of Iraq's second city involved a long march down deserted streets carrying a hundred and twenty pounds on his back.

Soon his company was moved along to a small town a few miles away and garrisoned in a fort just off the town centre. It was time to win hearts and minds. Life was split into four. Guard duty. Patrol. Rapid Reaction Force. And time off. Trev got the idea of hearts and minds. He made a few Iraqi pals and soon had a good deal in place whereby he would give then a few dollars to get their mums to cook up a curry. In the base there were boxes of unwanted rations which he would use to stuff his pockets with sweets and biscuits for the kids. Soon he cut something of a Pied Piper on the dusty streets. It didn't go down well with many of his colleagues who had little patience for anyone being nice to the Pakis.

And every evening the night air was filled with the sound of screaming coming from deep inside the base. When prisoners were taken during patrols, things had started to become more and more brutal. Lads started to compete with the levels of stick they dished out. It passed the time. It was a laugh. And later they would swap their stories. Trev looked to the men in charge to step in and make it stop. They didn't. Just like nobody had ever stepped in to make it stop when he had been beaten and beaten through the long, bleak years of his childhood. Where was Spiderman then? Where was Spiderman now? They had supposed to have been the good guys. Instead, every day saw many of the men around him turning into his stepfather as they got high on inflicting pain. And he was as helpless as he had once been as an abused five year old child. The rules of the Regiment were absolute. You stuck together. You did nothing. You said nothing. You followed the lead. End of story.

Whenever he could, he would jump forward to take the prisoners himself and get them back into the base before anyone had the chance to beat them.

But there was still screaming every night.

And with every passing day, the picture of those guys walking down from the plane in Kosovo faded away. He had wanted to become one of the guys who looked after the beaten and abused. He had wanted to avenge every beating he had ever received when there had been nobody to come through the front door to make it stop.

Instead he was a part of it.

And he was helpless yet again.

Screaming in the night.

Pumps and pipes.

Kick the Paki in the head.

Have a laugh.

Now he's a part of rapid reaction Force. Message on the wire. There are armed guys in the town square. Green uniforms and beards. Go, go!! They clatter across a plank bridge over a river that is little more than an open sewer. Spread out and cover. Brand spanking new Toyota 4x4's fresh from the showroom and the guys in green uniforms dodge into the mosque. Shouting and threats and the guys come out. They are terrified. Shaking. Staring death in the face. Not so the boss man. He feels like he is immune. The boss man starts to laugh. Mistake. Big, big mistake. The boss man is taken somewhere out of sight and soon the screams are worse than anything Trev has heard before. The other lads are banging the bad guys to the ground and the bad guys are jellied with terror. Nobody seems to speak English, but the message is clear enough. You can't do this. You shouldn't do this. We're protected. And a few of the lads are getting really hyper now because the bad guys have pockets stuffed with high denomination dollar bills. And in the

Toyota 4x4 there is a holdall stuffed with dollar bills. Someone reckons they are Iranians. Someone else reckons they must have been hired by the Americans. So? Several of them are getting a huge kicking now. Trev tries to take as many as he can himself. He tries to tell his mates not to take the wads of dollar bills. But his head is ready to burst with it all. Screaming and screaming and screaming. Just like he once screamed. Until the screaming behind the closed doors suddenly stops. And later nobody has anything to say about why the screaming stopped so suddenly. Except there are men with the wild eyes of men who have killed.

He was supposed to have been on the right side.

Aye right.

A few weeks later and he sat on a plane and gazed out at the impossibly beautiful green of the fields and woods of home.

Heathrow.

Leave.

A bad dream over.

There had been no combat. No chance to fight the forces of evil. Instead it had seemed as if some of his comrades had become the forces of evil. And things in his head started to get confused. Scenes from different movies became intertwined. There were the ones where he was being beaten and doing all the screaming and there was nothing he could do to make it stop. And now there were the ones when others were being beaten and screaming and there was nothing he could do to make it stop. The Regiment had supposed to be the place for a man who wanted to make the screaming stop. The maroon beret was supposed to have meant sticking up for the abused and the beaten.

Instead it had been about guarding oil infrastructure.

Instead it had been about screaming in the night.

It wasn't what had been written on the tin.

It had been confusing.

It had been bad.

And somehow his head was getting all scrambled up with it all.

After Iraq it became clear that the Regiment wasn't really what he was looking for in life. His last year in uniform was a time of winding down as he sneaked under the radar and got himself a place with the recruiting team. His final months were all about strapping excited kids into jump harnesses at country shows. He left with an unblemished record and a glowing testimonial for potential employers.

As he returned to Civvy street, he viewed his future with some optimism. Surely people would see him in a different light now. They had to. He had served four years in one of the world's most elite units and he had come through with flying colours. Nobody had told him he was no good in the Paras. Nobody had gone on and on about him just being a typical care home boy with a one way ticket to prison. More to the point, he had a piece of paper to prove it. The past was done with. The future would be a whole lot better. Surely everyone in Dumfries would see him in a completely different light. After all, he had done everything right. He had served his country with distinction. He had proved that he could thrive in the very toughest of environments. He had passed all the tests and jumped through hoops and out of planes. Now he would finally be treated with some respect.

Aye right.

Once upon a time, the kind of high hopes that Trev returned home with might have been justified. It is hard to think that the men who survived the carnage at Arnhem were ever treated with anything but the very highest of respect by the communities they returned to. By the time the lads from Goose Green came home, things had changed. We have one who stands outside Mark & Spencer in Dumfries selling the Big Issue. Let's just say that he doesn't exactly do a roaring trade.

Trev sooned the hard way that being a veteran of one of our much vaunted elite units is no kind of guarantee to a smooth and successful life. Quite the opposite in fact. If all the wannabe small town hard men had wanted to have a go at him before he joined up, they wanted it twice as much when he got home. Now he was an even bigger scalp to claim. A target. A more general view was that the fact that he was an ex Para who had served in Iraq meant that it was pretty damn certain that he was a dangerous nutter. Give him a wide berth. He's dangerous. Be careful about taking him on in the workplace. I mean after all, there are health and safety issues. Duty of care and all that. I mean, what would happen if he just flipped and kicked off? Steer well clear. He's dangerous that one. Bloody dangerous. He was bad enough when he was just an out of control care home boy. Imagine what he's like now! Should be locked up, so he should.

Deadly Paratrooper.

My oh my, don't we all just love our tabloid stereotypes.

None of these negative reactions had any kind of positive effect on Trev's increasingly scrambled brain. By now there were all kinds of images and flashbacks competing with each other in a frantic, chaotic waltz. Suddenly he was far too wired all the time. He just wanted a normal life just like any young man, but every time he went out on the town it seemed there was always some drunken nutter who wanted to go to war with him. Fights and brawls and trips to the police station. The police made it very clear what they thought of him. He was a threat. He was a potential danger to society. They told him they were watching. Always watching.

This wasn't how it was supposed to be. He had come home expecting to be shown some respect. Instead everyone seemed to be treating him like Peter Sutcliffe. Deadly Paratrooper. Worse still, everywhere he looked it seemed that there were abusers who could do what they liked and nobody seemed to care. Just like they hadn't cared when his stepfather had beaten him. Just like they hadn't cared when the Iraqi prisoners screamed and screamed in the heat of the desert night.

Right and wrong seemed to be all mixed up and nobody seemed to be bothered. Everywhere he went there seemed to be a squad car waiting around the corner. And yet all over the world the bad guys were allowed to deal drugs and beat children and abuse children and torture prisoners and there was never anyone willing to step up to the plate to make it stop.

No Spiderman, no Batman, no James Bond.

I won't dwell on all the stuff that came next as I am very much aware that this is a public document and Trevor is adamant that he has no wish to be anonymous. There was a site foreman who bullied his Polish workers with an unending stream of racism and violence. When Trev told him to wrap it up, the guy decided to have a go. It didn't end well for the foreman.

Red mist.

Over the recent years Trev has fought his one man war against a selection of drug dealers and abusers. He says that he likes nothing more than to abuse the abuser. Hero of the community? Out of control nutter? Lone Ranger or vigilante? Don't ask me. I'm just the guy hitting the keyboard. Like I said before, we had some pretty heated ups and downs when he decided to turn my fiction into real life. Through it all, Trev has always known that all is not well with his brain. He is frank about it. His memory is like a sieve and when something winds him up he loses the plot very quickly.

And believe me, when he loses the plot it is a pretty fearsome sight.

It isn't like he hasn't asked for help. On numerous occasions he has knocked on the doors of the mental health service and warned people that his brain is so scrambled up that he is worried that he is going to kill someone. This honesty didn't get him very far. Most of the time people freaked out and got him out of the building as quick as they could. Health and safety. Duty of care. Risk management. Deadly Paratrooper.

The one man vigilante stuff was never going to end well and it didn't. He was beaten and stabbed and arrested and locked up. They came for him mob handed. They outnumbered him. And yet they never managed to put him down and keep him down. The odds always stank and yet he constantly defied them. Mini versions of Goose Green played out in the alleyways of the schemes of Dumfries. Dark. Vicious. Brutal. And all the character building he had received care of his stepfather and the Parachute Regiment just kept on kicking in. Trevor is one of those guys who have no concept of the idea of being beaten. You would probably have to cut his head off to keep him down, and even then it wouldn't be a done deal. Sound familiar? Arnhem? Goose Green?

Aye right.

At last he got the opportunity to leave town and he took it. A new town meant leaving all his history behind. He doesn't go out now. He keeps himself to himself and with luck the wannabe hard men in his new town won't get to hear that there is an ex Para in their midst. Those who revel in tabloid stereotypes would be surprised at his flat. It is as clean as a new pin and filled with well looked after plants. Everything is polished and in its place and Trev is at pains to be the perfect host.

Thankfully his brain is finally on its way to being as well ordered as his new flat. A few months ago he was referred to Combat Stress and they now see him regularly. They finally provided a door that wasn't slammed in his face. They took him seriously when he told them that he was worried that he might kill someone. They are working with his GP and he is now taking medication that has calmed him down a lot. His sense of right and wrong still burns as brightly as ever, it just doesn't morph into the kind of red mist that will see him packed off to HMP Shotts until he is a middle aged man. The people at Hollybush House have told him that he is the first case where it appears that the flashbacks are caused by the memory of feeling helpless to intervene as prisoners were being abused. They have of course had guys who were on the wrong end of it, mostly care of the Japanese and Chinese. And they have had guys who have dished it out all the way from the internment camps built to tame the Mau Mau to the fortified bases of Ulster to the dusty cellars of Iraq and Afghanistan.

And of course they have found Trev to be one of the complicated ones where childhood trauma has been liquidised up with combat trauma to create a knotted brain that takes a whole lot of unpicking. As I write, I feel optimistic that the people at Hollybush House will indeed loosen the knots. I also like to think that when the great public read this and watch Trevor in the documentary that will hit the TV screen on Armistice Day, they will maybe be willing to drop their prejudices and cut him some slack. Oh sure, he's a handful, but if you take the time to look hard enough you will find a fine young man. The Parachute Regiment has already proved that when his energy is harnessed in a positive way he can achieve and contribute much.

Oddly enough, the situation Trev has found himself in having hung up his maroon beret reminds me of a similar dilemma faced by many devout Christians we have met in the course of our work at The First Base Agency. These are old fashioned people of faith who go to church on a Sunday and feel that they should do would they can to help those less fortunate than themselves. Thirty years ago, there would have seemed nothing at all unusual in this. And of course they would have been widely respected for their good work. Now many of these traditional Christians say that they try to avoid telling anyone about their faith. It has become a thing to be wary about going public with. Why? How can this be? It is all down to the behaviour of a minority of ultra 'born again' Christians who the public has come to see as religious nutters. Like many other minorities, they have given the majority a bad name that it doesn't remotely deserve. All football fans are not football hooligans. All teenagers are not drug taking, binge drinking, wheelie bin burning, foul mouthed Neds who threaten pensioners and breed like rabbits. All Muslims are not card carrying members of Al Queda. The list goes on and on. Sadly tabloid editors have learned over recent years that you can sell papers by the truckload by fanning the flames of public fear and outrage at the behaviour of small wacko minorities and thereby vilifying whole sectors of the community. As a result, many have come to fear and detest groups who were hitherto liked and respected: teenagers, Christians, veterans of our elite regiments.

For many centuries the British Army has offered a place of sanctuary for lads like Trev who have survived childhoods we prefer not to think about. The Army takes their anger and turns it into something positive. In many cases, these are the young men who have the determination and heart to make it all the way into our elite Regiments. And when the very hardest questions have been asked, these Regiments have never let us down, no matter how bad the odds, no matter what cost they have had to pay. There are few armies in the world who can match our track record in this, probably none. It is the public that has changed and the tabloid media must accept a large part of the responsibility for this. Just because a veteran has been in the Paras doesn't mean that he is a semi psychotic nutter who presents a threat to the community. That wasn't the way we treated the men who survived Arnhem and it shouldn't be the way we treat the ones who leave the elite combat regiments now. Of course, there will always be a minority who will live up to the tabloid stereotypes. Those who Trev saw adorning their walls with Swastika flags and revelling in beating the hell out of 'ragheads'. But these men are a minority and they will always be so and they should be treated as such.

Obviously the Army will always have to wire up the circuit boards of our elite soldiers rather differently than the rest of us. After all, these are the guys we want to stand up there on the wall when the Barbarians reach the gates. This makes it completely unacceptable when we then use the new politically correct protocols and procedures of health and safety and risk management and duty of care as an excuse to lock the doors of help to these men.

Thanks largely to Combat Stress, Trev has come an awfully long way over the last year and hopefully he still has far to go. He is the first to admit that he has done some pretty bad stuff in his one man war against the kind of abusers who have blighted his life. Now that his brain is more ordered, he has found a calmness that has made him much more grounded. It should never have taken him so long to find people willing to help him instead of showing him the door and then locking it.

'Deadly Paratrooper!'

A silly tabloid headline barely worth the chip paper it was printed on. The good news is that is exactly how Trevor sees the cutting in his scrapbook now. He sees it for what it is. Contemptible.

The sooner the rest of the community see it in the same light the better.

**FOREWARD**

**Lieutenant General Sir Alistair Irwin KCB CBE**
**President Veterans Scotland**

One of the inevitable consequences of war, conflict, call it what you like, is that there will be a roll call of human casualties. When that word, casualties, is mentioned we tend to form an image in our minds of the crumpled figures of men killed in action and of those who are physically wounded in some more or less grievous way. These wounds are easy for all to see, in the case of those who lose limbs or who are disfigured, permanently so. For those who suffer these wounds and for those who stand ready to help and support them, the situation is obvious and the remedy, if not simple or pain free, is at least relatively easy to understand and pursue.

This cannot be said for those who suffer another, invisible, form of wound. This is the wound which enters the brain and which at its worst can consume the whole body, the whole life, of the victim. It is not marked by a scar or by a missing arm but by behaviour and internal anguish. To complicate matters further the evidence of the wound may not come to anyone's attention, least of all the victim himself, until some unexpected time long after the events that insidiously and silently inflicted the wound in the first place.

We may imagine, for example, a platoon of soldiers engaged in the grisly business of retrieving and burying the bodies of men shattered in battle. We may try to put ourselves in the shoes of troops who come upon the gruesome remains of women and children murdered in a bout of ethnic cleansing. We may even be able to guess what it is like to experience the noise, blast and shock of incoming enemy fire over a protracted period, perhaps watching as our best friend, our mate, sinks mortally wounded to the ground in front of us. If we imagine these things we may not be surprised to learn that some of these soldiers will have been psychologically wounded by their experiences and that one day they will relive the horrors and will need help. It is a wound that once was called shell shock and has now come to be called Post Traumatic Stress Disorder (PTSD).

This disturbing collection of stories starkly illustrates the effect that PTSD has had on three former soldiers, all of whom served in the Army at different times over the last 30 or more years and who still suffer from the consequences. Few readers will be unmoved by these soldiers' tales, which for them have all the reality and factual accuracy of something that happened just a minute ago. However PTSD and the natural passage of time can often have the effect of distorting the fact in a man's mind and I hope that Don, Trevor and Willie, the subjects of these stories, will not take it amiss if I assure those readers with no military experience of their own that these men's recollections of life in barracks and on operations could not fairly be regarded as a generally accurate picture of the British Army at work and at play. The point of course is that for Don, Trevor and Willie what they remember *is* reality and they have to deal with it on a daily basis. Thanks to the work of the Defence Medical Services, of the NHS and but most especially of the charity sector, it is not now a burden that they have to bear on their own, though very many still slip through the net. I am proud to associate myself with the aims of this thought-provoking book (though not with some of the details of army life and action that it portrays) and do so in the hope that it will encourage a greater general understanding of this terrible phenomenon, PTSD, and ever more generous support for those organisations which are there to help those who suffer from it.

## THE FIRST BASE AGENCY VETERANS PROJECT

The First Base Agency is a drug and alcohol information and support centre based in Dumfries. We are a small, independent charity and for six years we have seen at first hand the havoc that drug and alcohol addiction can wreak. We support families affected by a loved one's drug and alcohol problem. We issue food parcels to people who find themselves in a bad place. And we give talks to thousands of school children every year to try and steer them clear of the misery of addiction.

Over the last few years we have seen a growing number of veterans trying to drive away their demons via the bottle or the needle. Several of these men have sought help only to find long waiting lists and closed doors. So it was that we decided to establish a new project to try and help our local veterans. Late in 2008 we received funding from the Scottish Government via Veterans Scotland to make this project happen.

One of the goals of our project is to help to raise public awareness of the difficulties that so many of our ex servicemen face once they leave the forces. This is the background to this short book. Several thousand copies will be made available to the public, all free of charge. We hope that this can help in a small way to make things better for the many thousands of veterans whose minds are still locked into the terrible times and events they have lived through and witnessed.

The First Base Agency
6 Buccleuch St
Dumfries
DG1 2AH

01387 279680

www.first-base.org

**AUTHOR'S NOTE**

I have now been writing novels for over ten years and this is my fifteenth book. I am a fiction writer and I make absolutely no claims to any great literary merit. Most readers tell me that my books are page turners which keep them up deep into the night. I also seem to attract a goodly number of readers who hardly ever pick up a book. Since I have been working at The First Base Agency, I have produced three books for the charity. Although these have been fictional stories, the lives of the characters have been based on the real life experiences of those who have walked through the doors of the Agency seeking help. My job was to try and give the reader an insight into how essentially good people can find themselves travelling some very dark roads as a result of what are initially relatively small mistakes. How does someone become a heroin addict? Why does a young person go off the rails? What does it look like when cannabis unravels a youngster's brain?

The feedback we have received suggests that I have been relatively successful in achieving this. It was on the back of this success that I suggested producing a short book made up of three fictionalised stories of men who have had a terrible time having left the forces. The idea was that the reader should know that even though all the names and places in the stories in the book are fiction, the story itself is a true account. As things have turned out, only one of the veterans whose stories I have tried to tell wanted to be anonymous. This is the second story: Don. Willie and Trevor had no wish to be anonymous.

All three men have participated in the project for one reason only – they hope that this book might in a small way ensure that the veterans of the future will not have to suffer what they have suffered. In short, they are still infused with a sense of duty; they are still looking out for their comrades.

This has been the hardest thing I have ever written by a country mile. I have come to realise that there is really no pressure in writing fiction. This has been an altogether different ball game. The three guys whose stories I have done my best to tell are fine men indeed. Proud and courageous. They have been to some very bad places and seen and done some bad things. I hope that no reader underestimates the guts it must have needed for them to put their experiences out on public view. This is a different kind of courage to the courage they once displayed whilst serving their country, but bloody brave all the same.

They deserve huge respect and I hope they get it.

Way back in the 1930's Christopher Isherwood wrote these words in his novel 'Goodbye to Berlin' (It eventually morphed into the film Caberet.)

'I am a camera with the shutters open, quite passive; recording not feeling'

This pretty well describes how I have tried to approach the task of writing this book. You should know that this is not intended as a history. I have done no cross referencing or checking. That is not what this is about. My job is simply to try to put the feelings and memories of the guys onto the page. Sometimes a writer needs to be a sponge. We should draw stuff in and then squeeze it back out without adding anything. I have to admit that I fell down on one element of the Christopher Isherwood quote: the 'not feeling' part. I won't pretend that listening to the guys was easy. You would have to be cold fish indeed not to be pretty rattled by what they have gone through.

To be frank, it has felt like a heavy responsibility. Writing fiction is all well and good and it doesn't matter a great deal if I make a mess of it. This has been very different. The three guys have trusted me to get it right and I hope I haven't let them down. If I have, I can promise that it wasn't for the lack of trying. Time will tell I suppose.

No doubt there will some who will ask what remotely qualifies me to try and write these stories. A fair point which I will try to address. Over the last ten years I have met all manner of people whilst researching my various novels – IRA and UDA men, drug dealers, drug users, police officers, asylum seekers…. It is a long and varied list. I hope that somewhere along the way I have developed some skill in reflecting real life. Have I ever been in a war zone? Yes. Have I ever been under fire? No. have I ever been a part of anything remotely like the guys in the book? Yes. I was in the Leppings Lane End at Hilsborough in 1989. Does it still haunt me? Of course it does, but I am lucky for the memories of what I saw that day have never burrowed into my brain like a plague rat, but I have learned enough to know that you should never say never.

Above all else, this is a subject that has made me angry. It has made all of us at The First Base Agency angry. Really angry. I have no wish to go into the rights and wrongs of the wars our soldiers are fighting as I write. That is not what this is all about. However if Governments decide to send our soldiers into harm's way for what ever reason, they surely have an absolute duty to look after them once they come back home. Instead, what we have seen at first hand that the State is penny pinching when it comes to giving our veterans what they need. An eighteen month wait to see an NHS psychiatrist? This is is more than a mere disgrace. I doubt if there is a word in the dictionary to describe what it is. Disgrace to the power of ten. An NHS psychiatrist once explained to me that an average case of a guy with combat stress requires ten appointments to make his life more liveable. How much for an appointment? £100. An average bill of £1000 to make a life more bearable. And yet we are making our veterans wait for eighteen months!

It doesn't wash and it shouldn't wash and hopefully the public are going to get more and more angry and vocal about it. The recent Government U turn regarding the Gurkhas is ample evidence that public pressure can hit the mark. Politicians are very good at telling bus that there is no money and of course the nation is pretty strapped at the moment. However there are some issues which absolutely demand priority and this is one of them. Were the Government to swallow some of its pride and cancel building the Media Centre for the 2012 Olympics and re-allocate the cash to looking after veterans, then there would be enough in the kitty for years to come. So what is the bigger priority? Pampering a few journalists for a fortnight or looking after the men who have been broken whilst fighting for their country. We mustn't buy into any of the talk of there not being enough money. The Government spends over £600 billion of our money every year. All they need to do is re-allocate some of this. It should be a no brainer and every one of us needs to keep kicking at the shins of the politicians until they do the right thing.

Sir Alistair has given me a ticking off for being so forthright about this. After all, this book would never happened had we not been awarded funding from the Scottish Government via Veterans Scotland. A fair point. Maybe I **am** biting the hand that feeds! However, thanks to the gallantry and sacrifice of many generations of our soldiers, we Brits still enjoy the right to speak our minds freely and I am duly claiming it. I should however find time to commend the Scottish Government for finding the money to open up Veterans First Point in Edinburgh, a really terrific project. Having said that, I must also point out that demand for the services at Veterans First Point is growing fast and all of a sudden there is a waiting list which is steadily growing. So come on guys, get out those pens and write more cheques!

A common denominator in all three stories is a charity called Combat Stress. This is a brilliant organisation that does fantastic work. Another excellent new project is Veterans First Point in Edinburgh. Right now the number of cases both of these organisations are handling is going up and up. Which of course means waiting lists are getting longer and longer. Our message to the politicians is very simple. There should be no waiting lists. There is no need for there to be any waiting lists. If these organisations need more money to make sure they can help our veterans quickly, then give them the money. It is as simple as that. Write the cheque, write it now and don't penny pinch. And if that means a few journalists working out of a Portacabin in 2012 then so be it.

I hope these stories give you some sort of an insight into the dark world so many of our veterans live in. If they do, then that has little to do with me. I am just the guy who does the typing. All credit should go to Willie, Don and Trevor. Please try and do what you can to ensure that the courage they have shown in stepping up to the plate is rewarded.

www.ingramcontent.com/pod-product-compliance
Lightning Source LLC
LaVergne TN
LVHW041237150826
845673LV00008B/2416

* 9 7 9 8 7 5 1 5 6 5 6 6 4 *